Rising Before the Start Line

Rising Before the Start Line

Lessons from Medicine, Purpose, and Quiet Leadership

Ajay Ovhal

COPYRIGHT

RISING BEFORE THE START LINE

This book is a work of non-fiction based on the author's personal experiences. Names, locations, and identifying details have been changed where necessary to protect privacy. Any resemblance to actual persons or events is coincidental unless explicitly stated.
This book was created with the assistance of AI-based language tools (including ChatGPT, OpenAI) for editing support, language refinement, and structural guidance. All ideas, experiences, interpretations, and final editorial decisions are solely those of the author.
The views expressed in this book are the author's own and do not represent the views of any institution, organization, or government body.
Medical Disclaimer:
This book is not intended to provide medical advice, diagnosis, or treatment. The information shared is for educational and inspirational purposes only. Readers should consult qualified professionals for medical concerns.
ISBN: 978-93-5626-012-2
Publisher: Ajay Govindrao Ovhal, India
Printed in India

Dedication

In loving memory of my brother, Vijay,
whose belief in me never wavered,
whose presence shaped my thinking,
and whose absence taught me the depth of resilience.

To my parents,
who gave me roots strong enough to stand firm
and wings honest enough to grow without losing myself.

To my wife, Deesha,
my partner in life and purpose,
whose quiet strength carried me
through both achievement and grief.

To my children, Deep and Abhinha,
who remind me every day
why integrity, courage, and compassion matter.

And to all those who walked with me—
teachers, mentors, friends, students, patients,
and well-wishers—
this journey belongs to you as much as it belongs to me.

Author's Note

This book was never planned as a project.
It grew slowly, over years—through conversations, memories, silences, and moments that refused to fade.

Rising Before the Start Line is not an autobiography written to list achievements.
It is a reflection on becoming—
becoming disciplined before becoming successful,
becoming ethical before becoming visible,
becoming resilient before becoming confident.

Every chapter in this book is rooted in lived experience: the uncertainty of early years, the pressure of medical training, the responsibility of public service, the courage to build institutions from nothing, the pain of loss, and the quiet strength drawn from family, mentors, students, and patients.

I have written this book primarily for young doctors, students, and professionals who begin their journeys without privilege, visibility, or shortcuts—those who often feel they must first *prove their right to dream.*
If this book offers reassurance that sincerity, consistency, and character still matter, then it has served its purpose.

The voice, values, decisions, and experiences in these pages are entirely my own. At certain stages of writing, I used a modern language tool to assist with refining expression, improving clarity, and maintaining narrative flow—much like one would work with an editor. The ideas, judgments, interpretations, and final form of this work remain authentically mine.
If these pages resonate with you, challenge you, or quietly accompany you during a difficult phase, I consider that the highest reward.

This is not the end of a story.
It is simply a pause—to reflect—before continuing forward.

— **Dr. Ajay**

Contents

PROLOGUE — Before the Journey Began

Some journeys do not begin with ambition.
They begin with observation.

Before the degrees, before the titles, before Marvel, before classrooms and corridors filled with students—there was simply a boy watching the world carefully, trying to understand where he belonged in it.

I was born into a family that did not have excess, but had values.
Education was not inherited—it was earned.
Stability was not assumed—it was built.
Dreams were not loudly announced—they were quietly protected.

I grew up seeing discipline before comfort, effort before reward, and responsibility before entitlement. My parents did not speak often about success, but they lived its prerequisites every single day. In that environment, I learned early that life does not owe you outcomes—it responds only to sincerity.

Medicine entered my life not as a glamorous aspiration, but as a serious commitment. It promised dignity, service, and purpose—but it also demanded sacrifice. As the years passed, I realized that becoming a doctor was not about mastering textbooks alone. It was about understanding people, systems, suffering, and oneself.

Long before I built clinics or departments, I learned something essential:

If you want a different life, you must first become a different person.

This book is not a celebration of achievements.
It is a reflection on becoming.

Becoming disciplined when comfort was tempting.
Becoming calm when circumstances were chaotic.
Becoming ethical when shortcuts were available.
Becoming resilient when life delivered loss without warning.

It is also a story of people—
mentors who shaped my thinking,
students who refined my purpose,
patients who taught me humility,
family who carried me when I faltered,
and a brother whose belief in me continues to guide my steps, even in silence.

Marvel Clinic did not rise from concrete and glass.
It rose from years of unseen effort, difficult decisions, quiet perseverance, and unwavering values.

Government service did not shape me through authority, but through accountability.
Teaching did not elevate me through titles, but through responsibility toward young minds.

This book traces that journey—from decision to discipline, from struggle to structure, from loss to rebuilding, and from individual effort to institutional vision.

The chapters that follow do not promise inspiration on every page.
They promise honesty.

Because real journeys are rarely dramatic.
They are steady.
They are demanding.
And they are shaped—one decision at a time.

This is the story of those decisions.
And this is where the journey begins.

CHAPTER 1

The Decision That Changed Everything

Some turning points arrive quietly.
They do not come with thunder, applause, or a spotlight.

They arrive as a single sentence in a newspaper, a line on a notice board, or a whisper of possibility that only a hungry mind can hear.

For me—a young man from rural Maharashtra—that moment came when **PG-CET** was introduced for the first time.

In that instant, without ceremony, a doorway opened.
A doorway out of predictability.
Out of limitations.
Out of the narrow lanes of destiny that most people from backgrounds like mine were expected to walk.

Before that moment, I had seen life closely at the **Primary Health Centre** level.
I had seen doctors working tirelessly with limited tools.
I had seen how talent suffocated under the weight of restricted opportunities.
I had seen how dreams were often buried beneath family responsibilities, financial constraints, and the unspoken expectation that boys from rural areas should "settle early."

But something within me refused to settle.

There was an unrest—a quiet fire that sparked
every time I saw a patient suffer because of lack of infrastructure…
every time I opened a textbook and realised how vast the medical world truly was…
every time I imagined a life where I could grow, build, create, and innovate.

So when PG-CET was announced, I did not see it as an examination.
I saw it as **escape velocity**—

a chance to rise above the gravitational pull of circumstance,
a chance to build a life different from everything I had known,
a chance to become the kind of doctor I had always envisioned:
skilled, independent, disciplined, and impactful.

At that time, most of my peers were preparing to settle into government service postings, seeking security and predictability. Many encouraged me to avoid the uncertainty of competitive exams.

"Why take the risk?" they asked.
"Why work so hard when you already have a path in front of you?"

But I understood something deeply:

If you want a different life, you must make a different choice.

On the evening the PG-CET news reached me, I felt something shift internally.
There was no dramatic moment—
just a calm, steady conviction rising in my chest:

This is my chance.
And I will not waste it.

That night, I made a promise to myself—not spoken aloud, not written in any diary, but engraved firmly in my mind.

I would give everything I had.
I would study with absolute sincerity.
I would push through exhaustion, loneliness, fear, and self-doubt.
I would not stop until the dream became real.

And so began the journey—
a journey that would reshape my character, forge my discipline, and

eventually give birth to something far larger than I could have imagined:

Marvel Clinic.
A transformed dermatology department at **GMC Latur**.
A life of purpose crafted through relentless effort.

But every great story begins with one moment.

For me, it was this—
a quiet decision,
a simple sentence on a notice board,
a young man whispering to himself:

"I must change my life."

And thus, the journey began.

CHAPTER 2

The Furnace Of Determination

Success does not arrive with a loud announcement.
It grows silently in the corners of a small room, under a dim yellow tube light—inside the mind of a young man who decides that his life cannot continue the way it is.

When PG-CET was announced for the first time, I understood one thing with startling clarity:

This was the only doorway wide enough to escape the limitations of my circumstances.

Life at the PHC meant forever adjusting, compromising, and accepting that growth would be slow and unpredictable. For the first time, the system had opened a fair pathway—one where merit mattered more than background.

I knew one truth:
If I wanted to change my life, I had to earn it.

So I locked myself into a disciplined routine—one that would later become the blueprint for everything I built in life.
I studied **12–18 hours every single day**.
No breaks.
No excuses.
No celebrations.
No distractions.

It was not glamorous.
It was not inspiring to witness.
It was simply **necessary**.

I broke my days into long, intense blocks of study—medicine, dermatology, anesthesia, microbiology, pharmacology—each subject read and revised with the pressure of survival.

There were no external motivators.
Only internal hunger:

> A better life.
>
> A better career.
>
> A future built by choice, not chance.

Some days, the letters in the books blurred from exhaustion.
Some days, self-doubt tried to whisper that I wasn't good enough.
Some days, I wondered whether the reward would truly justify the suffering.

But every time doubt rose, **discipline answered**.

And with discipline came a powerful transformation—
I stopped depending on motivation.
I started depending on routine.

That habit of relentless consistency would later define everything I created:
Marvel Clinic, the restructuring of the Dermatology Department, the systems I built in GMC Latur.

Small victories kept the fire alive—
solving a difficult MCQ set, finishing a subject revision, understanding a tricky concept.
These tiny sparks fueled the furnace.

I did not study to top the exam.
I studied because I knew I had to change my destiny.
PG-CET was not an examination—it was a bridge to a life I had only imagined until then.

When the results finally came, they were not just numbers.

They were **proof**—
that discipline is the highest form of self-belief,
that consistency is the strongest force in personal transformation.

The furnace had shaped me.

The boy who once feared limitations had now discovered his greatest strength:

the ability to outwork any obstacle.

CHAPTER 3

Choosing Dermatology Against The Trend

Counselling day is supposed to be exciting.
But for me, it felt like standing at a crossroads with hundreds of voices pulling in different directions.

Medicine. Surgery. Orthopedics. Pediatrics.

Everyone around me seemed to be running toward the same few "prestigious" branches, as if career success was measured only by how difficult or dramatic the work looked from the outside.

But I had never lived according to the noise around me.
I had always lived by clarity.

A senior professor's words guided me like a compass:

**"Choose a branch that matches your personality.
The branch should fit your life—
not the other way around."**

And when I finally listened to my own instincts, the answer became unmistakable.

Dermatology felt like home.

Not because it was glamorous—
back then, it was far from it.

Not because it promised quick money—
if anything, surgical branches were considered more lucrative.

I chose dermatology because it aligned with the kind of human being I was.

1. A Social, People-Oriented Personality

I enjoyed interacting with people, guiding them, and being present in society.
I was never the kind of doctor who wanted to disappear into a 36-hour emergency shift, buried inside ICUs and operation theatres.

Dermatology offered something rare—
the time and mental space to maintain social connections, contribute to community life, and stay engaged with people.

For me, that mattered deeply.

2. A Life Beyond Work

I valued balance, not burnout.

I wanted a career where I could still read, travel, pursue hobbies, exercise, spend time with family, and continue evolving as a human being.

Dermatology allowed that—
a field with depth at work, and breadth in life.

3. Not Obsessed With Money

Many around me chose surgical branches because of perceived higher income.

But I was never guided by money.
I was guided by meaning, skill, and long-term growth.

I had learned early:

If you focus on mastery and sincerity, money eventually follows.

Dermatology allowed me to live by this belief.

4. A Self-Reliant Field With No Superspeciality Burden

One of the most practical advantages was this:

Dermatology is a terminal branch.

No superspecialization required.
No additional 3–5 years of MCh or DM.
No emotional or financial burden of more examinations.

I could start working, learning, growing, and becoming self-reliant immediately after post-graduation.

This clarity saved me years of struggle and allowed me to build Marvel Clinic much earlier, while many others were still navigating endless training cycles.

5. A Branch That Rewards Calmness and Precision

My temperament naturally matched dermatology—
observant, patient, analytical.

I enjoyed pattern recognition, microscopic detail, long-term relationships with patients, and the blend of medical, surgical, and aesthetic practice.

Dermatology matched **who I was**, not who society expected me to be.

The Road Very Few Took

When I finally wrote **“Dermatology”** on the choice sheet, there was no applause.
There was no crowd following me.
But inside, there was a deep, quiet certainty—
the silence a person feels only when they have made the right decision.

That single choice, taken against the trend, shaped every chapter that followed:

> the department I would later build at GMC
>
> the laser expertise I developed
>
> the mastery in pediatric dermatology
>
> and ultimately,
>
> **the birth of Marvel Clinic**

Even today, when students ask me how to choose a specialty, I tell them:

**“Choose a branch that respects your personality and your life.
A career is not a badge—
it is a lifestyle.”**

Dermatology wasn’t the obvious choice.
It was the authentic one.

And authenticity is the foundation on which great journeys are built.

CHAPTER 4

Residency: Where Skills and Leadership Were Forged

Residency is meant to test endurance, intellect, and emotional strength.
For me, it became something deeper.
It became the phase where leadership, empathy, and courage first took shape.

The 7 a.m. to 1 a.m. Rhythm

My days began before sunrise and ended well past midnight.
OPDs, procedures, ward calls, theory sessions, emergencies—each day carved out the dermatologist I was becoming.

I didn't merely complete duties.
I owned them.

I took extra calls, stayed back for difficult cases, supported juniors, and stepped forward whenever help was needed. I wanted to learn, and I wanted to serve—fully and sincerely.

A Doctor Who Cared for the People Behind the Cases

During ward rounds and cross-consults, I interacted not only with patients, but also with colleagues who were silently carrying the weight of residency.

Simple questions like:
"Jevan zale ka?"
"Thodā ārām kar."
"Mi aahe—kahi asel tar sang."

were often enough to build trust and camaraderie.

Residency can be isolating.
I wanted to make sure it didn't feel that way.

Raising a Voice — Building MARD at LTMMC

Early in my residency, I recognized a pattern of systemic neglect faced by resident doctors:
unsafe call rooms
broken washrooms
lack of drinking water
absence of security
rising violence against on-duty doctors

Most accepted these conditions silently.
I couldn't.

I helped establish the MARD (Maharashtra Association of Resident Doctors) branch at LTMMC, giving residents a unified platform and a voice.

We advocated for:
security deployment around wards
safe rest rooms
basic sanitation
drinking water facilities
humane working conditions

It was not rebellion.
It was reform—rooted in dignity and logic.

Loved by Nurses and Class IV Workers

I treated everyone—senior consultants, nurses, ayahs, ward boys—with equal respect.

I shared meals, asked about their families, appreciated their work, and stood up for them when needed. Over time, this created something invaluable: a quiet but powerful support system.

In moments of chaos, they would stand beside me and say:
"Doctor saab, tumhi jaa… ami ahot tumchya barobar."
(Doctor sir, don't worry—we are with you.)

That sentence carried a strength no textbook could ever teach.

The Night That Changed Me Forever

One incident from residency remains etched in my memory.

A 65-year-old Sardarji was admitted with an adverse drug reaction. He appeared stable through the day. But during evening rounds, something subtle unsettled me—he seemed more drowsy than expected.

My instincts warned me: *Something is wrong.*

I raised the alarm immediately. Medicine was informed. Urgent investigations were sent.

Within hours, the picture became clear:
elevated serum ammonia
deranged liver enzymes
rapid progression toward hepatic encephalopathy

Outside, rain battered the hospital grounds. Inside, relatives gathered—nearly a hundred by midnight.

Through the night, I coordinated with seniors, anesthetists, and nurses. Fluids, vasopressors, oxygen—every possible measure was taken.

At 7 a.m., despite all efforts, the patient passed away.

Exhausted and emotionally drained, I stepped out of the ward. Four or five strongly built relatives approached me. For a brief moment, fear tightened my chest—a young resident, a large gathering, and a death.

Before I could speak, one of them folded his hands and said softly:
"Doctor saab, tussi raat bhar mehnat kitti...
sāḍe pitājī nahi bache, par tussi apnā farz nibhaaya."

(Doctor sir, you worked the entire night.
We lost our father, but you fulfilled your duty.)

In that moment, I learned a truth that has stayed with me forever:
When intentions are pure and efforts are sincere, people recognize it—even in their grief.

Residency Shaped More Than Skills

By the end of residency, I had gained far more than clinical competence. I had developed:
courage in crisis
clarity in decision-making
emotional steadiness
leadership
humility
compassion

Residency did not just prepare me for dermatology.
It prepared me for life.

I entered residency as a hardworking student.
I emerged as a doctor with values, vision, and an unshakable sense of purpose.

CHAPTER 5

Mentors Who Shaped My Vision

No one becomes who they are alone.
Every meaningful journey is shaped by a few extraordinary people whose wisdom becomes part of one's DNA.

For me, that guiding presence was **Prof. Dr. Hema R. Jerajani**, my Professor and Head of Department—a mentor whose influence extended far beyond academics.

The Mentor Who Led With Light

She was not a teacher who treated knowledge as possession.
She believed in something far more powerful:

"If you have knowledge, let others light their candles in it."

In an environment where insecurity often encourages people to withhold what they know, she was open, transparent, and generous. Students, visiting consultants, residents, researchers—everyone was welcomed. She personally demonstrated instruments, discussed procedures, shared books, and opened doors.

Knowledge, to her, was meant to circulate.

The Observations That Shaped Me

I observed her closely—not consciously at first, but deeply.
How she managed time with precision.
How she spoke with grace.
How she organized the department like a well-calibrated system.
How she multitasked without chaos.
How she promoted research quietly but consistently.
How she led without raising her voice.

These observations became lessons that later shaped my own leadership.

Ahead of Her Time

In 2007, when most colleges still relied on OHP transparencies, she introduced PPT-based seminars.
She adopted digital cameras, computers, and technology-driven documentation long before it became routine.

Her message was clear to me early on:

"Change is not to be feared. It is to be embraced."

That philosophy later guided my own decisions—whether it was adopting lasers, digital systems, or designing modern clinical spaces at Marvel.

Opportunities That Expanded My Horizon

She never limited learning to OPDs and wards.
She sent me to work with the Research & Development department at Unilever, exposing me to corporate dermatology, formulation science, and product development.

These opportunities were rare.
She offered them because she valued sincerity and potential.

A New Way of Teaching

Long before problem-based learning became official policy, she practiced it naturally.
Her classes were discussions, not monologues.
She taught us **how to think**, not merely **what to remember**.

Confidence Where I Needed It Most

Coming from Marathwada, I carried a quiet insecurity about my accent.
She dissolved it with one sentence:

"People across countries have different tones and pronunciations. It has nothing to do with intelligence."

That sentence freed me.
It allowed me to speak, teach, and lead without hesitation.

Standing Beside Me During MARD Leadership

When I became actively involved in MARD as General Secretary and faced administrative scrutiny, she never distanced herself.

Her response was calm and firm:

"He is sincere, committed, and performs excellently in the department."

That support strengthened my spine for every institutional battle that followed.

Dr. Rajeev Joshi — Precision, Discipline, Destiny

After being shaped by her leadership and philosophy, another mentor profoundly influenced my academic foundation—**Dr. Rajeev Joshi**, one of India's most respected dermatopathologists.

The Wednesdays That Defined My Foundation

Every Wednesday during residency was sacred.
For two of my three years, I was in charge of dermatopathology.

I prepared the most challenging slides—
blistering disorders, adnexal tumors, granulomatous diseases, obscure infiltrates.

Sitting across from him, slide by slide, confusion turned into clarity.

These were not teaching sessions.
They were masterclasses in reasoning.

A Mentor's Dinner — And a Life-Changing Direction

After my MD exams, he invited me for dinner.
Away from microscopes and exams, I asked him:

"Sir, where should I settle?"

He paused and said:

"Settle where you come from.
Where people need you the most.
Doctors from Mumbai and Pune will not settle in Latur.
But you will belong there."

That sentence aligned my career with my roots.

Two Mentors, One Vision

One mentor taught me how to **lead people**.
The other taught me how to **read patterns**.

Together, they shaped the doctor, teacher, and leader I became.

Mentorship is not instruction.
It is inheritance.

And I carry that inheritance every day.

CHAPTER 6

Choosing Marathwada: A Decision of Purpose

Every young doctor eventually faces a question that shapes an entire future:
Where should I build my life?

For most of my peers, the answer was straightforward—
Mumbai, Pune, or other major cities with strong infrastructure, abundant opportunities, and established medical ecosystems.

My decision, however, was not guided by glamour, competition, or convenience.
It was guided by purpose.

I followed my mentor Dr. Rajeev Joshi's advise given during a quiet dinner:

"Settle where you come from.
You will grow there."

Those words did not feel like advice.
They felt like direction.

They aligned perfectly with my instincts, my upbringing, and my desire to contribute meaningfully rather than blend into metropolitan competition. That conversation became my compass—one that pointed me back to Marathwada.

Understanding the Need

At that time, Marathwada had almost no MD dermatologists.

Patients travelled long distances for even basic skin care. Skin diseases were stigmatized, mismanaged, or ignored. Many were misdiagnosed or treated inadequately due to the absence of specialist care.

I knew these realities intimately.
I had grown up among these people.
I had witnessed their struggles firsthand.

And I understood something simple, yet powerful:
Where scarcity is highest, impact is greatest.

Choosing Purpose Over Popularity

My decision surprised many friends and colleagues.

"Why return to Latur after becoming a dermatologist?"
"Why leave Mumbai when opportunities are limitless?"

But I was not looking for a crowded lane where I would be one among hundreds.

I wanted:

- meaningful work
- genuine service
- balance for family life
- space for personal growth
- the satisfaction of building something from the ground up

I did not want to be another dermatologist in Mumbai.
I wanted to be **the dermatologist who made a difference in Marathwada**.

A Decision That Defined the Future

With calm certainty, I told myself:

"I will return to Marathwada.
I will settle in Latur.
I will serve where I am needed the most."

It was not the easy choice.
It was the right one.

That single decision planted the seeds for everything that followed:

Marvel Clinic

modernization of dermatology in Latur

development of the GMC Dermatology Department

postgraduate seats

laser dermatology excellence

pediatric dermatology referrals

leadership during COVID

and the rise of a regional center of excellence

Everything grew from this one point of purpose.

The Courage to Go Home

Most people leave their hometown to chase success.

I did the opposite—
I went home to create it.

Not just for myself,
but for the thousands who would eventually walk into Marvel Clinic,

for the students who would train under me,
and for a region that needed modern dermatology far more than it realized.

I did not choose Marathwada because it was easy.
I chose it because it was waiting for me.

This decision became the heartbeat of my journey.

CHAPTER 7

Marvel Clinic 1.0: The 360 Sq Ft Beginning

Some dreams begin with applause.
Some begin with resources.

But the dreams that endure—
the ones that eventually become legacies—
often begin quietly.

In small rooms.
With borrowed courage.
And with the unexpected kindness of people who arrive at exactly the right moment.

Marvel Clinic 1.0 was born that way.

Choosing Latur — A Decision of Heart and Vision

After finishing my residency, I did not look toward Mumbai or Pune, where most specialists naturally gravitated.
I looked homeward—toward Latur.

It was a city I understood instinctively:
cultured and respectful people,
a strong educational environment,
a growing business ecosystem,
and a region finding momentum under the leadership of Shri Vilasrao Deshmukh.

Dermatology was underserved here.
Patients travelled long distances for basic care.
Skin diseases were often ignored, mismanaged, or stigmatized.

The region needed someone trained, updated, and committed.

My mentor Dr. Rajeev Joshi's words echoed within me:

"Settle where people need you the most."

With that clarity, the destination was set.
Latur was not a compromise.
It was a calling.

The Search for a Clinic — Help Arrives in Human Form

Finding a place to start a clinic is difficult when you have limited money, no contacts, and no map for the journey ahead.

At that moment, destiny intervened—through people.

The first was **Dr. Bharat Sonawane**,
Professor of Pathology at SRTR Medical College, Ambajogai, and a close family friend.

Without hesitation, he said:

"Chala, Latur la jauya."
("Come, let's go to Latur.")

He took my father and me in his own car—not as a courtesy, but as genuine support for a young doctor standing at a crossroads.

In Latur, he introduced me to **Dr. Umesh Kanade**,
a respected pathologist and owner of Omsai Laboratory.

Dr. Kanade didn't merely offer advice.
He took me by the hand and said:

"Chala doctor, mi dakhavto."
("Come doctor, I'll show you.")

Lane by lane.
Building by building.
Corner by corner.

We searched together—not as professionals conducting a transaction, but as mentors and well-wishers investing belief.

This was not assistance.
It was goodwill in its purest form.

Finding the 360 Sq Ft Space

After hours of searching, we found it—
a 360 sq ft room near the bus stand.

It wasn't large.
It wasn't luxurious.

But it had location.
Accessibility.
Possibility.

Standing inside the empty room—with bare walls, dusty floors, and a single window—I didn't see what it was.

I saw what it could become.

A beginning.
A seed.
The first step toward a lifelong dream.

The ₹10 Lakh Decision — And the Man Who Made It Possible

Dreams, however, do not turn into clinics without courage—and capital.

For a middle-class doctor, ₹10 lakh felt enormous.

What if patients didn't come?
What if the EMI became unbearable?
What if everything failed?

At this crucial moment, another extraordinary person entered my life—
CA Shri Jugal Baheti.

I approached him with hesitation, unsure whether to proceed.

He listened quietly and said:

"Take the loan.
Start properly.
Don't worry about repayment.
You have MD Dermatology.
You will do well.
Believe in yourself."

It was not financial advice.
It was faith.

And that faith endured.

For the next eighteen years—until today—he has never charged me a single rupee in professional fees.
He guided every financial decision, planned strategies, connected me with banks, and stood beside me like a pillar.

Many times, I wondered:
Do such people truly exist?
Do good intentions attract good people?

They do.
When one walks with sincerity and humility.

Building Something Small, With Big Intent

I designed the 360 sq ft space with care:

clean partitions,
good lighting,
organized workflow,
and an atmosphere that felt trustworthy.

I bought essential instruments—not extravagant, but precise and purposeful.

Within that tiny room, I created a complete clinic built on structure, professionalism, and warmth.

23 September 2007 — The First Day

Marvel Clinic opened.

Five patients arrived.

To some, five might seem insignificant.
To me, they meant everything.

They represented trust.
They represented hope.
They represented a beginning.

I spent time with each patient.
Explained gently.
Diagnosed carefully.
Treated ethically.

I wasn't rushing.
I wasn't competing.

I was building.

The Birth of the Marvel Culture

Inside that 360 sq ft space, Marvel's identity was born:

empathy before medication
time before crowd
counselling before prescription
ethics before popularity
sincerity before shortcuts

Patients noticed.

Slowly.
Quietly.
Steadily.

They returned.

More Than a Beginning

Marvel Clinic 1.0 was not just a clinic.

It was the soul of everything that followed.

A small room.
A modest setup.
A young doctor with a dream.
And a circle of people whose kindness made it possible.

Some journeys are built on money.
Some on power.

But the journeys that last
are built on good intentions—
and the good people they attract.

That is how Marvel Clinic was born.
Not merely as a clinic,
but as a quiet miracle shaped by sincerity, humility, and human kindness.

CHAPTER 8

The Inauguration: When Dreams Took Shape

Here are days when life moves quietly, building in the background without announcement.
And then there are days when everything you have worked for suddenly stands before you—real, tangible, and filled with meaning.

For me, the inauguration of Marvel Clinic 1.0 was one such day.

Preparation — A Small Space, A Big Moment

The 360 sq ft clinic had been cleaned, polished, and made ready.

Fresh flowers marked the entrance.
A simple rangoli welcomed visitors at the door.
Soft yellow lights warmed the walls.
Charts, instruments, and books were placed with care.

It was not grand.
It was not luxurious.

But it was mine—
built with belief, designed with intention, and carried on the shoulders of countless small sacrifices.

The Guests Arrive

As the time approached, people began to gather—each one representing a chapter of my journey.

Among those present were:

Dr. Shirole, Dean, MIMSR Medical College

Dr. Santosh Kavthale, renowned Cardiologist

Dr. Potdar, Deputy Director of Health Services

Respected members of the Latur medical fraternity

Family, friends, mentors, colleagues, and well-wishers

All the coordination had been handled meticulously by **Dr. Sandip Kavthale**, whose thoughtful efforts ensured everything ran smoothly. He personally invited the dignitaries and managed logistics so I could remain present in the moment.

My parents sat in the front row—
my father steady and composed,
my mother already emotional, though trying hard to conceal it.

The Lamp That Marked a Beginning

The lamp was lit.
The ribbon was cut.

Applause filled the narrow corridor.

For a few moments, everything felt unreal.

The space that had lived only in imagination was now alive.
This was no longer an idea or a plan.

This was the first physical form of a dream that had grown silently over years.

Called to Speak

After the formalities, the anchor announced:

"Now, we request Dr. Ajay Ovhal to share a few words."

I stood slowly.

My palms were cold.
My heartbeat louder than usual.

I walked to the small podium and glanced at the board behind me—**Marvel Clinic**, shining quietly in blue and white.

Then I looked at the audience.
At my mentors.
At my friends.
And finally… at my parents.

In that instant, memories surged forward:

PG-CET struggles

ST bus journeys between Ambajogai and Latur

Sleepless duty nights

Emotional breakdowns

The hardest days of residency

Unexpected kindness from seniors

Steady support from friends

The tense decision to take a ₹10 lakh loan

The fear of failure

The courage to trust myself

The search for this small 360 sq ft space

And the people who stood beside me—silently, steadfastly

Years of effort, doubt, sacrifice, and persistence collapsed into a single moment.

My throat tightened.
My eyes filled.

A Mother's Tears

I tried to blink the tears away, but they came faster.

I looked at my mother.

Her eyes were already wet.

Those tears carried decades of:
silent worry,
quiet sacrifice,
unwavering faith,
and pride never expressed loudly.

One guest leaned toward another and whispered softly:

"This must be his mother."

Everyone understood.

No explanation was necessary.

A Speech Made of Silence

I held the microphone.

For a few seconds, no words came.

The hall was silent—not with discomfort, but with respect.
Everyone felt the weight of the moment.

Then, slowly, I began.

I thanked:

- Dr. Shirole for gracing the inauguration
- Dr. Santosh Kavthale for his encouragement
- Dr. Potdar for lending dignity as a senior government representative
- Dr. Sandip Kavthale for organizing the event with care
- Dr. Bharat Sonawane and Dr. Umesh Kanade for their support in finding the clinic space
- Every mentor, friend, and colleague who had shaped my journey

But my most heartfelt gratitude was reserved for my parents.

They did not speak.
They did not move.

They simply looked at me—
with the quiet pride that needs no words.

My mother wiped her tears softly.
My father nodded—measured, composed, deeply fulfilled.

A Dream Blessed

That day, Marvel Clinic was not merely inaugurated.

It was blessed.

Blessed by tears.
Blessed by gratitude.
Blessed by humility.
Blessed by the presence of those who mattered.

Everyone present saw more than a clinic.

They saw the beginning of a legacy—
built not on money, but on meaning.
Not on luxury, but on ethics.
Not on glamour, but on grit.

Marvel Clinic 1.0 was no longer just a 360 sq ft space.

It had become the heartbeat of my purpose—
the first step in a journey that would one day inspire thousands.

CHAPTER 9

Marriage, Partnership & Stability

A life built on discipline and ambition becomes stronger when balanced with companionship.
For me, marriage was not just a milestone — it was the beginning of partnership, emotional stability, and shared purpose.

Meeting Deesha — The Calm That Balanced the Storm

In 2008, after the intense years of MBBS, residency, and establishing Marvel Clinic, I entered a new phase of life — marriage to **Dr. Deesha**, MD Anatomy.

Deesha brought with her:

quiet confidence

a gentle temperament

a disciplined academic mind

and unwavering emotional grounding

Where I had fire, she had calm.
Where I had unstoppable momentum, she had thoughtful steadiness.
Together, we became a balanced team — complementing, supporting, and elevating each other.

A Partnership of Two Different, Yet Perfectly Aligned Worlds

As I expanded Marvel Clinic and joined GMC Latur, my schedule became a demanding blend of:

OPD hours

procedures

emergency calls

administrative responsibilities

departmental development

academic leadership

Yet Deesha never saw herself as a spectator to my life.

She was a partner in every sense.

She handled her responsibilities as an Anatomy faculty member with grace and professionalism, while simultaneously giving me the emotional stability I needed to pursue large goals.

She became the quiet pillar behind my visible achievements.

The Strength of a Home That Believed in Each Other

Every doctor knows the chaos of balancing marriage and a medical career.
But Deesha and I created a rhythm — a harmony — where both careers flourished without one overshadowing the other.

She understood:

the long OPDs

the unpredictable emergencies

the stress of building a department

the pressure of loans

and the dual demands of government service plus private practice

She never complained.
She simply stood by me — gently, silently, strongly.

Her presence created stability.
Her belief created confidence.
Her calm created clarity.

Where many relationships struggle between ambition and domestic life, we built a partnership rooted in shared sacrifice, mutual respect, and deep understanding.

Two Different Strengths, One Shared Direction

Deesha's temperament brought invaluable qualities into my life:

patience

empathy

thoughtful decision-making

balanced perspective

quiet wisdom

These traits softened the sharper edges of my intense, highly disciplined personality — creating a life that was not only productive, but peaceful.

Meanwhile, my commitment inspired her growth in academics, research, and teaching excellence.

Our strengths did not overlap.
They completed each other.

The Foundation of Family Life

As years passed, we built a home where love and discipline coexisted effortlessly.

Between OPDs, duties, and conferences, there were:

shared meals

long conversations

quiet evenings

and the comfort of companionship after exhausting days

When our children arrived, they added joy, creativity, and purpose to our home.
Life became fuller, warmer, and even more meaningful.

The balance between:

personal life

professional ambition

and mutual growth

remained the anchor of our journey.

The Silent Support Behind Marvel's Rise

As Marvel Clinic grew busier, Deesha continued to support every step — taking care of home responsibilities, academic duties, and the emotional weight of a growing practice.

Later, she played a significant role in Marvel's digital presence, especially through the YouTube channel, which brought medical education and patient awareness to thousands.

Behind every milestone of Marvel, there is a quiet imprint of Deesha — her calmness, her stability, her steady reassurance.

Marriage — The Anchor Behind Ambition

I often say:

"My discipline built my career,
but my family gave it meaning."

Deesha didn't just marry a doctor.
She partnered with a dream.
She believed in a man building something from scratch.
She stood beside me without hesitation.

Our marriage was not about perfection.
It was about alignment —
two people choosing each other every day,
choosing patience,
choosing growth,
choosing partnership.

Marvel Clinic may have been founded by me —
but the life around Marvel,
the stability behind Marvel,
and the peace within Marvel
came from the home I built with Deesha.

Together, we transformed a life of ambition into a life of purpose.

CHAPTER 10

Joining GMC: a Call Of Duty

Building a private practice brings satisfaction.
But serving in a government medical college brings purpose.
For me, this purpose arrived through a single phone call —
a call that would shape the next two decades of my life.

The Call From Dr. Solepure — A Teacher's Faith in His Student

One day, I received a call from my respected UG teacher, **Dr. Solpure**, a senior physician known for his sharp mind and deeply ethical approach to medicine.

His voice carried the same warmth I remembered from medical school.

"Ajay, GMC Latur needs you.
You must join us.
Your people need your service."

There was no hesitation in his tone.
No ambiguity.
No formality.

It wasn't a request.
It was a **call of duty**.

Something shifted inside me.

A teacher had not merely asked —
he had **entrusted** me with responsibility.

I didn't know then that this phone call would eventually shape:

the dermatology department at GMC

the PG seats

the workflows and systems

the academic culture

and the lives of countless students

At that moment, I felt only one thing —
honour.

Balancing Two Full-Time Careers

Accepting the offer meant embracing an extraordinary challenge:

Government service + Marvel Clinic
Two full-time responsibilities.
Two different worlds.
Two different demands.

But I didn't see it as a burden.
I saw it as:

a chance to serve the poorest

a chance to teach budding doctors

a chance to elevate dermatology in a region that lacked it

a chance to build something larger than personal success

My schedule became intense:

Morning GMC OPD

Afternoon Marvel OPD

Evening GMC calls

Night private consultations

Administrative duties in between

Days blurred into nights, and nights became new days.
But I kept going —
with the same discipline and sincerity that had shaped every step of my journey.

The 1.5-Year Marathon of ST Bus Travel

In the initial months, I was still living in Ambajogai.

So I travelled daily:

Ambajogai → Latur → Ambajogai
on the ST bus,
in scorching summers, pounding monsoons, and freezing winters.

Every day was a test of endurance.

I would:

reach GMC for OPD

work at Marvel

return to Ambajogai late at night

sleep exhausted

wake up again before sunrise

This routine wasn't just difficult —
it was **character-building**.

I learned: patience

time management

resilience

physical and mental toughness

the ability to serve without complaint

This phase polished me more profoundly than any textbook ever could.

Stepping Into GMC — A Department Without Structure

When I joined GMC Latur, dermatology was almost invisible.

There was:

- no proper OPD structure
- minimal instruments
- no IPD
- no ward
- no schedules
- no patient records
- no team
- no formal academic activity

Dermatology existed on paper —
not in practice.

With a shortage of faculty, I was soon given HOD charge as an Assistant Professor.

Instead of worrying, I began building.

Building the Department Brick by Brick

I created structure where none existed.

I:

- designed OPD flow
- reorganized patient rooms
- started dermatology IPD services
- procured essential instruments with minimal budget
- established a dressing room
- created patient case sheets
- developed academic schedules
- trained residents and interns
- built trust with Medicine, Surgery, Pediatrics, OB-GYN, and Orthopedics
- introduced evidence-based dermatology to the college

Slowly, a neglected department became a **functional, respected specialty**.

Why I Was Different

People join government service for many reasons.

I joined with:

impeccable discipline

respect for systems

a teacher's heart

a desire to uplift the region

and a fierce commitment to doing things the right way

Students noticed.
Colleagues noticed.
Other departments noticed.

I was not there to mark attendance.
I was there to **build**.

The Roots of Leadership

During those early years, I unknowingly laid the foundation for:

PG seat battles

laser procurement

COVID leadership

administrative reforms

and a strong departmental culture

None of this was visible yet.

I was simply doing what I had always done:

working sincerely,
working silently,
working relentlessly.

Not for credit.
Not for praise.
But because I believed:

**"If something is worth doing,
it is worth doing with full integrity."**

A Choice That Defined a Lifetime

Joining GMC was not a career move.
It was a **lifetime commitment** —
to service, to teaching, and to the people of Marathwada.

It became the second pillar of my professional identity —
the one rooted in **purpose**, not profit.

Marvel Clinic made me a practitioner.
GMC made me a leader, a teacher, and a servant of society.

Two worlds.
One mission.

A life lived in service and sincerity.

CHAPTER 11

The Hardest Routine: 1.5 Years Of ST Bus Travel

Before Marvel Clinic became busy…
before GMC found its structure…
before leadership roles, PG seats, and departmental reforms…
there was a chapter of my life that tested me more than any exam ever could.

A chapter of pure endurance — lived in silence, without applause, without recognition.
A chapter only middle-class dreams truly understand.

The Dual Life — GMC in the Morning, Marvel in the Evening

When I accepted the teaching post at GMC Latur, my life instantly became a balance between:

- government service
- patient care
- department building
- and my private practice

But there was one complication —
I was still living in **Ambajogai**.

Which meant daily travel.

Not by car.
Not by train.
Not in comfort.

But by **ST BUS**.
Every. Single. Day.

Ambajogai → Latur → Ambajogai.

This became my life.

The Daily Journey — A Test of Mind and Body

I travelled through:

- scorching summers
- torrential monsoons
- winter chills
- overcrowded buses
- dusty roads
- unpredictable timings

The bus wasn't just transport —
it became a **moving classroom**, a **meditation chamber**, and often, a **test of willpower**.

Some days there were seats.
Many days there weren't.
Some days I stood the entire journey.
Some days I rushed straight from the bus stand into OPD.

I would leave home early, return late,
and somewhere in between…
I built my resilience.

The Routine That Polished Me Like Fire

My day looked like this:

5:30 am — Wake up
6:30 am — Catch ST bus
8:30–9:00 am — Reach Latur
9:30 am onwards — GMC OPD / wards / teaching
3:00–3:30 pm — Move to Marvel
4:00–9:00 pm — Private OPD
9:30 pm — Catch ST back
11:00–11:30 pm — Reach home
12:00 am — Sleep

And then… repeat.

Every.
Single.
Day.

No shortcuts.
No weekends.
No rest.

This wasn't a schedule —
it was a **furnace**.

And like metal in fire,
I was being shaped.

The Psychological Battle — Without Complaints

Traveling in an ST bus daily is not glamorous.
It doesn't build social media status.
It doesn't create followers.
It doesn't attract admiration.

But it builds:

patience

humility

grit

mental strength

the ability to work without comfort

the discipline to serve without excuses

Many people in difficult phases complain.
But I didn't.

I kept going — silently, consistently — because I believed:

**"If I want to lift this department,
I must first lift myself."**

People Wondered How I Managed

Colleagues asked:

"Ambajogai? Daily?"
"By bus? In this heat?"
"How do you manage?"

I simply smiled.
I wasn't seeking sympathy.
I was seeking progress.

This quiet strength resonated with many —
nurses, staff, and young residents.

They saw a teacher who didn't preach discipline.
He **lived** it.

The Moments on the Bus — Where Clarity Grew

Strangely, the ST bus became a place of reflection.

In those bumpy rides, in the hum of the engine, I often planned:

- improvements to GMC OPD
- how to organize the dermatology ward
- which instruments to procure
- how to restructure clinic workflow
- how to manage finances
- how to grow Marvel step by step

I wasn't wasting time.
I was **designing my future**.

Small Incidents That Stay Forever

There were days when:

- I sat squeezed between villagers discussing crops
- I stood near the door holding the iron handle
- I got drenched in monsoon before reaching OPD
- I shared wada-pav or bhaji with fellow travelers
- I felt exhaustion deep enough to hurt

But every day,
I **showed up**.

This built something powerful inside me —
an endurance no gym, no classroom, no motivational talk ever teaches.

The End of the Bus Chapter — But the Beginning of Growth

After 1.5 years, I finally shifted to Latur.
Life became easier.
Routine became manageable.

But I never forgot those days.

Because those days made me:

- grounded
- strong
- empathetic
- determined
- unbreakable
- deeply connected to common people

Many successful people forget their struggle.
But I carried it with gratitude.

That ST bus did not just take me from Ambajogai to Latur.

It carried me:

from **uncertainty → direction**
from **pressure → clarity**
from **exhaustion → endurance**
from **young doctor → future leader**

This Routine Became My Secret Strength

Years later, when:

- the fight for PG seats began
- COVID demanded 24×7 leadership
- administrative battles piled up
- Marvel 3.0 construction tested my patience
- shifting clinics felt risky

I could handle everything.

Why?

Because I had already survived the hardest training of all —
the ST bus phase.

It shaped my identity in ways no degree ever could.

CHAPTER 12

Building The Dermatology Department At GMC: From Zero To Structure

When I first walked into the Dermatology Department at GMC Latur,
I did not find a department.
I found a room.

A room without structure.
A specialty without identity.
A service without recognition.

But what others saw as emptiness,
I saw as **potential**.

Just as I had converted a 360 sq ft room into Marvel Clinic 1.0,
I now had to convert a neglected corner of the college into a functioning specialty.

I didn't wait for someone to ask.
I simply began.

The Department That Existed Only on Paper

Dermatology was treated as a minor subject — almost an afterthought.

There was:

no formal OPD structure

no IPD

no instruments

no workflow

no dressing room

no ward rounds

no teaching schedule

no academic activity

Dermatology existed in name, not in practice.

Many would have accepted this.
Some would have worked minimally and gone home.

But I believed:

"If I have come, the place must grow."

The Assistant Professor Who Became HOD Overnight

Because of faculty shortage, I — an Assistant Professor — was handed HOD charge.

This could have intimidated anyone.
But to me, designation was secondary.
Responsibility was primary.

The department needed:

structure

service

training

identity

Someone had to take the first step.
I took all of them.

Creating OPD Flow — The First Building Block

I started by fixing the basics:

organised registration

a simple triage area

properly arranged waiting space

examination cubicle

documentation patterns

case sheets and follow-up formats

I created protocols so that the department did not depend on any single person.

A system was born.

Starting IPD — A Turning Point

Dermatology at GMC was almost entirely OPD-based.
But conditions like:

pemphigus

erythroderma

SJS/TEN

vasculitis

severe psoriasis

complicated infections

drug reactions

needed inpatient care.

I pushed for dedicated beds — and finally, Dermatology IPD services began.

I handled admissions, planned treatments, coordinated with Medicine, Pediatrics, Anesthesia, Surgery — and slowly, the perception changed:

From
"Dermatology is minor"
to
"Call dermatology — they will handle it."

Respect was not demanded.
It was earned.

Improving Equipment — Doing More With Less

Government budgets move slowly.
But I moved fast.

With minimal resources, I procured:

dermatoscopes

minor procedure kits

thermocautery

cryo therapy tools

magnifiers

biopsy instruments

emergency medicines

dressing materials

phototherapy support

Every item was:

clean,
functional,
organized.

Small improvements transformed patient care.

Building Interdepartmental Trust

In government medical colleges, departments survive on cooperation. I built relationships with:

Medicine

Surgery

Pediatrics

Obstetrics

ENT

Orthopedics

Ophthalmology

Burns Unit

I attended consults promptly, helped during emergencies, guided treatment plans, and followed up diligently.

Slowly, the image of dermatology changed.

We became **reliable**.

Teaching Becomes a Culture, Not a Task

I established:

- weekly seminars
- case presentations
- slide discussions
- histopathology reviews
- clinical spotting sessions
- bedside teaching
- journal clubs

Students who once considered dermatology a "short posting" began engaging sincerely.

Interns stopped bunking.
They started learning.
They respected the subject —
because they saw sincerity in the teacher.

The Legacy of Professionalism

I introduced:

- punctual OPDs

clean documentation

clear reporting formats

planned academic schedules

academic files

clinical audits

logbooks

structured departmental meetings

Residents began adopting these habits.
The department began functioning like a **mini-institute**.

People noticed.

A Foundation That Would Shape Future Victories

This period laid the groundwork for:

the battle for PG seats

equipment upgrades

interdepartmental respect

laser advocacy

academic recognition

COVID leadership

and the rise of GMC Dermatology as a respected unit

I didn't build the department in a day.
I built it **each day**, with quiet consistency.

I believed:

**"If you create a system that works,
your presence becomes a bonus —
not a requirement."**

From Nothing to Structure — A Silent Achievement

There were no awards.
No public appreciation.
No headlines.

But what I built was far more valuable:

A department that would outlive me.
A place where:

students learn

patients trust

colleagues cooperate

dermatology thrives

Every strong building needs a foundation.

At GMC Latur,
I quietly became that foundation.

A specialty that once existed only on paper
became a pillar of healthcare in Marathwada.

CHAPTER 13

Dr. Shrikant Gore: The Mentor Who Shaped My GMC Journey

Some meetings in life arrive without warning,
and yet they redirect the entire course of one's journey.

During my years at GMC Latur, I met many teachers, seniors, and colleagues.
But only one person became a mentor strong enough to shape my leadership, my thinking, and my very identity.

That man was **Dr. Shrikant Gore**.

The Day Courage Created a Connection

It began on a day charged with quiet unrest.

Interviews for selecting resident doctors had been scheduled, yet in an unusual and unfair deviation from tradition, the Dean did not invite any Heads of Departments. HODs—normally members of the college council for such interviews—felt insulted and sidelined.

Everyone sensed the injustice.
But no one dared to question it.

Among the candidates stood a young woman—seven months pregnant—competent, hopeful, and deserving. The Dean denied her selection solely on the basis of pregnancy.

Something within me refused to remain silent.

I was still an ad-hoc faculty member then.
Yet I walked into the Dean's cabin and asked, calmly and directly:

"Under which rule can pregnancy disqualify her?"

The room froze.

No one questioned the Dean publicly.
But I did—not out of aggression, but out of fairness.

In an adjacent cabin, behind a half-open door, sat a man observing everything quietly. A man who valued integrity over convenience, courage over silence.

That man was **Dr. Shrikant Gore**.

That evening, he invited me for dinner.
It was our first real conversation—the beginning of a mentorship that would quietly shape decades of my life.

He told me gently:

"Truth must be spoken, Ajay.
But spoken with strategy.
Courage is precious—learn to direct it."

That was the day a mentor entered my life.

The Man Behind the Reputation

In the corridors of GMC, Dr. Gore was often described as reserved, strict, and introverted—someone who had left private practice purely for teaching.

But I discovered the truth beneath the surface:

A deeply sensitive human being.
A scholar with clarity rare in government institutions.
A skilled orthopedic surgeon with sharp clinical judgement.
A man of rules, discipline, and order.
Exceptionally particular about cleanliness and systems.

Humble in manner, uncompromising in ethics.
Adored by students, respected across departments.

He appeared firm on the outside—
but was profoundly human on the inside.

A Mind Built on Systems, Precision, and Documentation

If I had to name one quality of Dr. Gore that transformed me permanently, it would be **clarity**.

Clarity in thought.
Clarity in systems.
Clarity in ethics.
Clarity in leadership.

He taught me:

> to read documents word by word
>
> to draft proposals with logic and justification
>
> to insist on flawless documentation
>
> to build systems that outlive individuals
>
> to separate facts from emotions
>
> to rely on written clarity rather than verbal assurances

His eye for detail was legendary.

During equipment procurement, he would check stretcher thickness with a screw gauge and even stand on it to test strength.
Specifications, for him, were sacred.

Through him, I absorbed:

rationality,
scientific temperament,
and the quiet dignity of humility.

Guidance During the Hardest Phase — Deesha's Terminations

When MPSC-selected candidates joined and Deesha was terminated three times within two years, I was deeply hurt and angry. I wanted to confront the Dean, to question the repeated humiliation.

Dr. Gore intervened softly.

"Do not fight temporary fires, Ajay.
Find a permanent solution."

Then he asked a question that struck at the core:

"Can you live away from your family?
Can they survive without you?
Such distances create frustration, addiction, strain.
Think long-term."

That moment changed everything.

Deesha and I decided she would pursue **DDV**—a stable, lasting academic path. That advice didn't just shape careers; it protected our family's future.

A Mentor Who Built Systems — And Clean Spaces

Dr. Gore believed discipline must be visible—even in the soil of an institution.

He would call me, and together we would walk through the most neglected corners of GMC—rear blocks, hostels, clogged passages.

He planned drainage systems.
Removed decades-old garbage.
Invited NGOs to participate in campus cleanliness.

Under his supervision, over **50 truckloads of waste** were cleared. We even created a **Miyawaki forest** inside the campus.

Leadership, he believed, must begin with hands-on action.

Uncompromising Ethics

When GMC revenue suddenly increased after computerisation, Dr. Gore sensed malpractice. Against resistance, he requested an audit that exposed financial irregularities in cash collection.

His message to me was clear:

**"If the system is clean,
you can sleep peacefully."**

For him, ethics was not an option.
It was identity.

He Saw a Leader Before I Saw Myself

One day he told colleagues:

"Ajay has the mindset of an institutional leader."

To test and nurture this, he recommended me as **In-Charge Dean**, even when senior professors existed. He convinced then-Dean **Dr. Rajaram Powar**.

When I hesitated, worried about seniority, Dr. Powar said words I never forgot:

**"The chair does not ask your age.
It asks for dignity.**

If you hold the charge, hold it like a Dean.
Documentation flawless.
Decisions calm."

That moment marked my true entry into leadership.

How His Guidance Shaped Marvel 3.0

Dr. Gore's influence extended beyond GMC into the foundation of **Marvel 3.0**.

From him I learned:

- meticulous planning
- turn-key project structure
- notarised, time-bound contracts
- stage-wise payments
- clear specifications to avoid disputes

Marvel 3.0 stands today **without a single conflict or litigation** because its foundation was built on these principles.

During construction, he even lent me **₹10 lakhs**—a gesture of trust and friendship I carry with deep gratitude.

He attended the inauguration and first anniversary of Marvel not as a guest, but as someone who had shaped its philosophy.

Kindness in Quiet Acts

His humanity revealed itself in small, unforgettable gestures:

- sending me with ₹5,000 to support the wife of a deceased Class IV worker organising Diwali breakfast for Class IV employees

promoting deserving Class IV staff to Class III posts

gifting a portable OT light to Dermatology when funds were unavailable

He taught me that leadership is **compassion in action**.

A Friend, Though of My Father's Age

Despite being my father's age, Dr. Gore became one of my closest friends.

He often told me:

**"Be a creator, Ajay.
Very few people build.
Most only consume."**

And another line he lived by:

**"Live like a human being—not like an organism passing through life.
Work with passion.
Work with intention."**

His philosophy was simple:

**"Do your work without expectation.
Do it for your own satisfaction."**

Guiding Me Through Grief

After I returned broken from the loss of my younger brother Vijay, Dr. Gore offered quiet strength. He spoke of impermanence, acceptance, and responsibility toward family.

His words helped me stand again.

The Inner World He Opened

He introduced me to:

rationality

scientific thinking

the philosophy of Ayn Rand

disciplined thought

and **Vipassana meditation**

On his recommendation, I attended the 10-day Vipassana course at Igatpuri—a turning point in my emotional and spiritual life.

A Life of Discipline and Excellence

Even before the retirement age of 64, Dr. Gore remained exceptionally active:

completed a high-altitude trek at 62

plays cricket at 68

immersed himself in modern farming

He was awarded **Best Medical Teacher** by the Director of Medical Education & Research—a recognition of a life lived with integrity.

Final Reflection — A Mentor Who Lives in the Systems You Build

Some teachers teach subjects.
Some teach skills.
A rare few teach how to think, lead, and live.

For me, Dr. Shrikant Gore was that rare mentor.

Even today, when I draft a note, design a system, take a calm decision, or walk through the GMC campus with responsibility, I feel his influence.

Marvel carries my name—
but in its foundation lies the quiet handwriting of mentors like **Dr. Shrikant Gore**.

CHAPTER 14

The Turning Point: The MPSC Interview and Becoming Associate Professor

Hard work does not always bring immediate rewards.
But when it does, it arrives with the quiet dignity of deserved recognition.

For me, that recognition came through the **MPSC interview**—an interaction that did not merely change my designation, but reshaped the future of dermatology at GMC Latur and, in many ways, across Marathwada.

The Need for a Permanent Post

By this time, I had already been working relentlessly at GMC Latur:

building departmental structure

creating OPD systems

starting IPD services

conducting OPDs sincerely

establishing academic routines

strengthening interdepartmental trust

Yet, I was still working on a **temporary post**.

Temporary posts come with limitations.
They do not allow long-term planning.
They weaken authority in administrative matters.
They make it difficult to fight for budgets, equipment, or PG seats.

And they keep the future uncertain—for both the department and the individual.

I did not want permanence for prestige.
I needed it for **power to build**.

Preparing for the MPSC Interview

I prepared for the MPSC interview the same way I approached everything in life—with discipline.

I revised:

- NMC and MCI norms
- departmental requirements
- government health policies
- dermatology guidelines
- administrative procedures
- and my own contributions so far

But more importantly, I prepared something deeper:

clarity of purpose.

I was not going to the interview merely to secure a job.
I was going to secure a future for:

- the dermatology department
- its patients
- its students

and its long-term growth

The Interview — A Question That Defined Everything

Inside the interview hall sat a panel of senior officials and subject experts—calm, experienced, and observant.

After routine questions, one senior panelist asked:

"Dr. Ovhal, you are already functioning as HOD on a temporary basis.
Why should we promote you?
Why should we give you a permanent post?"

It was not a confrontational question.
It was a test.

A test not of knowledge,
but of **vision.**

Without hesitation, I replied:

"Sir, a permanent post will allow me to contribute more.
Dermatology needs development—
equipment, structure, PG seats, and expansion.
If I am regularised,
I can build the department,
create opportunities for future faculty,
and secure the specialty's growth.
This is not only for my career,
but for the institution's future."

The panelists looked at each other.

This was not the answer of someone seeking comfort or security.
It was the answer of someone seeking **institution-building**.

It was ambition—but not for myself.
It was ambition for **Marathwada**.

Merit Rank 1 — The Moment of Validation

A few weeks later, the results were declared.

I secured **Merit Rank 1**.

Not second.
Not third.
First.

It was a moment of validation—quiet, profound, deeply satisfying.

Years of struggle, discipline, service, ST bus travel, silent work, and consistency had finally surfaced.

This was not luck.
It was earned.

Becoming Associate Professor — A New Phase Begins

With MPSC selection came:

- a permanent post
- seniority
- administrative authority
- decision-making power
- and institutional legitimacy

I could now:

- demand better equipment

push for budget allocations

fight for PG seats

formalise teaching programmes

and develop dermatology as a full-fledged specialty

This was not just a promotion.

It was **empowerment**.

Empowerment to build.
Empowerment to plan long-term.
Empowerment to change systems.

Dermatology at GMC Latur was no longer a marginal unit.
It had begun its journey toward becoming a centre of academic and clinical excellence.

The Home That Brought Stability

Professional stability also brought personal stability.

Deesha and I moved into a **Class I 2BHK quarter**—a simple home, but one that offered:

peace

proximity

time

warmth

and a sense of belonging

For the first time in years, life slowed down enough to breathe.

The ST bus chapter had ended—but it left behind resilience that would serve me in every challenge ahead.

A Promotion That Meant More Than a Title

Associate Professorship mattered not because it added a designation before my name.

It mattered because it added:

weight to my decisions

credibility to my proposals

strength to my voice

responsibility to my leadership

and momentum to departmental growth

This moment became the launchpad for everything that followed:

the battle for PG seats

laser procurement

paediatric dermatology expansion

Marvel Clinic transformation

and eventually, Marvel Institute

Every milestone ahead stood on this foundation—

the day I became Associate Professor through MPSC Merit Rank 1.

CHAPTER 15

The Nd:YAG Laser Battle: Light For The People Of Marathwada

Some battles in life are fought with swords.
Some with silence.
And some are fought with files in hand and fire in the heart.

My fight to bring the Nd:YAG laser to GMC Latur was that kind of battle —
largely invisible, rarely acknowledged, yet deeply consequential.

It was not about purchasing a machine.
It was about bringing light into the lives of patients who had known only limitation and neglect.

The Moment the Rule Hit Hard

One evening, sitting alone in my small departmental office, I opened the thick book of MCI norms.
I wasn't reading as an administrator.
I was reading as a doctor who wanted to build a future for his department.

My eyes froze on a single line:

> *"A minimum of two dermatology lasers is mandatory for initiating MD Dermatology postgraduate training."*

Two lasers.
Mandatory.
Not desirable.
Not optional.

I leaned back and closed my eyes.
The tube light flickered above, casting a dull glow over the file.

"So this is the first wall," I whispered to myself.

And then, instinctively, faces appeared before me.

A young man desperate to remove a tattoo so he could join the army.
Women hiding congenital pigmentary patches under layers of makeup.
Children whose parents travelled more than 150 kilometers hoping someone could treat a birthmark.
Labourers burdened by traumatic tattoos they wished to erase.
Young girls losing confidence to deep pigmentation that no cream could touch.

"How do I tell them we don't have the laser?"
"How do I explain that their hope depends on a file moving across tables?"

That night, I made a quiet promise to myself:

If MCI wants two lasers, I will bring them — not for inspection, but for these people.

From that moment onward, I was no longer fighting for equipment.
I was fighting for dignity.

Administrators Saw Cosmetics. I Saw Human Pain.

The next morning, I submitted the proposal for a Q-switched Nd:YAG laser.

The file barely moved.

It returned within a day, stamped with remarks:

"Cosmetic equipment."
"Not required in a government hospital."
"Unnecessary expense."
"Patients can go to private clinics."

I felt anger — not for myself, but for the casual dismissal of real suffering.

I carried the file from office to office, calmly answering every objection.

One administrator smirked and said,
"Doctor, it's a beauty treatment, no?"

I looked at him steadily.

"Sir, this is not beauty. This is treatment.
A tattoo prevents a young man from serving the nation.
A birthmark shatters a child's confidence.
Nevus of Ota is not cosmetic — it is medical."

I placed the MCI rulebook on the table.

"And without lasers, sir, we can never get MD Dermatology PG seats.
This is not a luxury.
It is compliance."

For the first time, the room fell silent.

Someone finally understood.

The File Became My Companion

The file moved forward inch by inch — and returned with twice as many queries.

"Explain wavelength."
"Justify Q-switched over diode."
"Provide comparative quotations."
"Is maintenance feasible?"
"Is it essential for government setup?"

Each query demanded time, science, patience.

I stayed late, drafting responses after OPD hours, after clinic, after family time had ended.
Some nights were exhausting.
Some days felt lonely.

But every time doubt crept in, I remembered the patients' folded hands and hopeful eyes.

That kept me going.

The Turning Point

The breakthrough came when I presented actual cases.

Not theory.
Not glamour.
Reality.

Photographs of dermal pigmentation.
Tattoo cases.
Congenital birthmarks.
Medico-legal tattoo removals.
Severe post-inflammatory pigmentation.

Patients from Latur, Nilanga, Udgir — people with nowhere else to go.

I said quietly,
"These patients don't have private options."

The committee room went silent.

For the first time, the administration didn't see a cosmetic laser.
They saw a bridge —
between rural patients and modern dermatology,
between neglect and dignity.

The file moved.

Sanction. Tender. Procurement.

Months later, approval came.

The Nd:YAG laser arrived — black, silent, powerful.

I touched it lightly.

Not because it was a machine,
but because of what it represented.

A promise kept.
A barrier broken.
A future unlocked.

The First Patient

The first patient was a young man rejected from army recruitment because of a tattoo.

He walked in with fear.
He walked out with hope.

Then came a child with a birthmark.
A woman with nevus of Ota.
A boy with traumatic tattoos.
A girl with deep pigmentation.

One by one, stories changed.

The laser was no longer equipment.
It became a symbol —
that government hospitals could be modern,
that Latur was no longer behind,
that Marathwada deserved excellence.

Not for Inspection — For Inspiration

No one saw the months of struggle.
The nights rewriting files.
The explanations.
The resistance.

But everyone saw the outcome.

For me, the Nd:YAG laser was not a trophy.

It was a message:

> *If your intention is sincere and your purpose is service,*
> *systems eventually bend.*

That first beam of light laid the foundation for the next great battle
—
the fight for MD Dermatology postgraduate seats.

And it proved one truth I would carry forever:

Change does not begin with permission.
It begins with conviction.

CHAPTER 16

The Fight For PG Seats: A Battle For The Future Of Marathwada

Some battles are fought on open fields.
Some on public stages.

But the battles that decide the future of generations are often fought quietly —
in file rooms, in dim corridors, in silent offices where a signature can change destiny.

The fight for MD Dermatology postgraduate seats at GMC Latur was not an administrative assignment for me.
It was a responsibility.
A promise.
And eventually, a legacy.

Because PG seats are not numbers.
They are doctors of tomorrow.
They are specialists for rural patients.
They are hope for Marathwada.
And they are the backbone of a department that wishes to outlive its founder.

To earn those seats, I had to walk through resistance, rigid policies, politics — and personal sacrifice.

The First Shock — The Missing Unit

The MCI norms were clear and unforgiving.

To apply for **three MD Dermatology seats**, a department must have:

1 Professor

1 Associate Professor

1 Assistant Professor

2 Senior Residents

Clinically, dermatology at GMC Latur was thriving — strong OPD, active IPD, growing referrals.
But structure matters more than effort in regulatory systems.

At that time, I was Associate Professor.
But one Associate Professor was not enough.
The second was missing.

Without a complete unit, the dream would remain locked.

This was not a missing form.
It was a missing limb.

Strengthening the Team — Growing Together

The Assistant Professor in the department was sincere and capable, but did not yet fulfil the publication criteria for promotion.

I could have waited.
I could have blamed the system.
I could have accepted delay.

Instead, I chose collaboration.

"If the department has to grow," I told myself, "we grow together."

I sat with my junior.
Guided research ideas.
Helped draft manuscripts.
Corrected references.
Ensured ethical submissions.
Followed timelines strictly.

Each accepted publication moved the department closer to eligibility.

I was not just building a unit.
I was building a colleague.
And in doing so, building the future.

The Shortcut I Refused

Just as dermatology neared completion of its unit, a tempting proposal arrived.

Another department — faced its own PG inspection issue.
They lacked one Associate Professor.

A suggestion was made:

"Promote Ajay to Professor now.
That will vacate the Associate Professor post in Dermatology.
We'll temporarily give that post to other department."

On paper, it looked efficient.
In reality, it was dangerous.

Once transferred, there was no guarantee the Associate Professor post would return to Dermatology.
And without that post, PG seats would collapse — not for one year, but possibly for a decade.

I refused.

I chose to delay my own promotion by a full year.

In that moment, I was not acting as an ambitious faculty member.
I was acting as a guardian of the department.

I told myself quietly:

Better I lose one year,
than Marathwada lose ten.

That decision defined my leadership.

The Year of Waiting

For an entire year, I remained Associate Professor despite being fully eligible for Professorship.

I continued:

OPD and IPD work

teaching

documentation

mentoring

strengthening systems

I did not wait with frustration.
I waited with purpose.

Because I knew — the moment the Associate Professor came in, the department would stand complete.

And only then would I move forward.

The Team Completes

Months later, the Assistant Professor fulfilled the publication criteria and was promoted as Adhoc Associate Professor.

Only then did I accept my own Adhoc Professor promotion.

I did not celebrate the designation.
I celebrated the team.

At last, Dermatology had a complete MCI-compliant unit:

1 Professor (eligible senior faculty)

1 Associate Professor

1 Assistant Professor

2 Senior Residents

Because that team was the foundation of the PG program we were about to gift to the institution.

The ₹10 Lakh Wall

With the unit ready, documentation complete, and inspections due — another obstacle emerged.

The college had to pay **₹10 lakh affiliation fees** for PG inspection.

The Dean refused.

"No budget."
"Later."
"Not a priority."

For me, this was not delay.
It was derailment.

Without payment, inspection would not happen.
Without inspection, PG seats would remain locked.

I did not argue emotionally.
I escalated systematically.

Taking the Fight Upward

When local administration becomes a wall, the only path forward is upward.

I took the entire documentation to:

DMER

MUHS

higher authorities

I explained clearly:

the department was ready

the faculty was complete

the region deserved PG seats

the obstruction was administrative, not academic

I did not complain.
I documented.
I did not dramatize.
I reasoned.

And the Directorate responded.

A letter arrived:

> *"The Dean shall release the affiliation fee immediately.*
> *Non-compliance will be viewed seriously."*

One letter.
One instruction.
The wall broke.

COVID — A Pause, Not a Denial

Just as everything aligned, COVID-19 struck.

All inspections were postponed.

Standing in the empty college courtyard, masked and silent, I felt the familiar whisper:

"Not again."

But destiny was not denying us.
It was preparing us.

During lockdown, I refined everything:

- documentation
- case records
- infrastructure
- registers
- OPD/IPD organization

I knew that when inspection arrived, dermatology would speak for itself.

Inspection — And a Historic Result

When inspectors finally came, they saw:

- discipline
- structure
- patient load

teaching records

complete faculty

Nd:YAG laser

clarity of vision

They did not just see a department.
They saw intent.

And then the letter arrived.

Three MD Dermatology Seats Sanctioned.

I held it quietly.

I thought of the year I delayed promotion.
The files.
The resistance.
The patience.

This was not my victory.

It was Marathwada's.

Completion of the Circle

Three years later, after the first batch passed out successfully, expansion became possible.

Another letter arrived.

Two more PG seats granted.

From zero seats
to three
to five.

This was not growth.
This was legacy.

A Department That Will Outlive Me

I did not start a PG program.
I built a department that will live beyond me.

I did not bring seats.
I brought opportunity, specialists, and dignity to a region that needed it.

And once again, the truth proved itself:

If intentions are pure
and purpose is service,
systems bend.

This chapter did not end with applause.

It ended with quiet pride —
the pride of knowing the future had been changed, permanently.

CHAPTER 17

The Brother I Carried In My Heart

Some people enter our lives like gentle breezes.
Vijay entered mine like sunlight — bright, warm, and impossible to ignore.

From the earliest years, it was evident that Vijay was different. He learned to read English even before formal schooling, absorbing words effortlessly, as if they were melodies. Teachers paused in disbelief. Parents smiled quietly, recognising brilliance without needing applause.

School toppers come and go.
Vijay remained one — always.

Examinations, competitions, scholarships — he rose with ease, not because he rushed, but because clarity came naturally to him. At sixteen, he made a decision that surprised many: he moved alone to Latur. Confidence was never taught to him. It lived in his bones.

He topped his twelfth standard with exceptional scores and earned admission into the prestigious **Institute of Chemical Technology (ICT), Mumbai**. Engineering was followed by **MBA Finance at JBIMS**, and soon after, professional roles at **BASF** and **ICICI**.

But Vijay's ambition never paused at borders.

He crossed oceans and completed his **Master of Science in Mathematical Finance at the University of North Carolina, Charlotte** — excelling in a program where even gifted students struggled. He joined **TIAA**, where he was not only respected for his intellect, but deeply valued for his ethics, warmth, and reliability.

All of this was achieved without inherited privilege.
Without shortcuts.
Without a safety net.

His success was built on discipline, ambition, and an unbreakable will.

My parents and I had stood as co-borrowers for his education loans, but Vijay repaid that trust many times over — through his achievements, his humility, and his unwavering gratitude. During the early, financially tight days of Marvel Clinic 1.0, he even contributed toward my marriage.

That was Vijay — a giver, a supporter, a pillar of our family.

The Year We Lived Together

When Vijay got his first job at BASF, I was completing my MD in Dermatology. We lived together in Mumbai for one year — a quiet phase that would later influence the digital backbone of Marvel.

Vijay introduced me to a new world:
Gmail,
search engines,
PowerPoint,
Excel formulas,
digital documentation,
data analysis.

With patient midnight lessons, he taught me Excel so thoroughly that I completed my dissertation without a statistician. But what he really taught me was modern thinking — clarity, efficiency, and structure.

The polished systems of Marvel, its digital workflows, and its organised ethos all carry Vijay's early imprint.

The Dreamer With a Family Heart

Vijay always thought big — not for status, but for growth. His dreams were collective. He imagined family trips to America, yearly reunions, shared memories across continents.

He helped everyone quietly — passports, visas, paperwork, guidance. No noise. No obligation.

And despite living thousands of miles away, he remained emotionally present. Almost every day, he would ask me:

"Bhau, aaj Marvel madhe kiti patients aale?"

Distance never diluted his involvement.

The Illness That Changed Everything

Despite a disciplined lifestyle — regular exercise, conscious eating, meditation, no addictions — Vijay began experiencing difficulty swallowing. Investigations followed. The diagnosis arrived like a thunderbolt:

Esophageal carcinoma, Stage III.

The earth shifted beneath me.

How could this happen to someone who lived with such care? Yet illness does not obey logic. Doctors spoke of long-standing silent reflux, possibly aggravated by emotional stress. I never allowed blame to enter my heart.

Only love.

Standing Beside Him in His Fight

When his condition worsened, I travelled to the United States and stayed for two months — through surgery, through uncertainty, through days when hope felt fragile.

Eventually, I returned to India, planning to go back soon.

But destiny chose otherwise.

Before I could travel again, the call came.
Vijay was gone.

I flew back with my father for the funeral — two men walking through the heaviest moment of their lives. A brilliant mind had gone silent.

But love does not vanish with breath.

Learning to Stand Again

Returning to India, I broke internally. Work felt distant. Dreams felt hollow. Life seemed paused.

Then a Buddhist teaching returned to me:

"Do not be broken by the death of those you love.
Carry their goodness forward.
Honor them by living fully."

Slowly, I began to rise — not because the pain left, but because life demanded presence.

My parents needed strength.
My sister Anjalee needed support.
Deesha stood beside me.
GMC needed leadership.
Marvel needed continuity.

Grief stayed.
But I learned to walk with it.

A Brother Who Never Left

Even today — after OPD hours, during difficult decisions, or when Marvel 3.0 glows under evening lights — I hear that familiar voice:

"Bhau… tu karu shakto."

And I know the truth.

Vijay did not leave.
He simply moved into a different room of my heart —
a room where love speaks without words,
where guidance arrives in silence,
and where strength is borrowed, again and again.

CHAPTER 18

Marvel 3.0: Rising After Loss, Rebuilding With Purpose

Marvel 3.0 did not begin as concrete, steel, or architectural drawings. It began as a quiet promise — a promise I made to myself, to my patients, and to the memory of a brother whose belief in me never wavered, even in the darkest hours.

This chapter is not merely about a building.
It is about rebuilding a life.

A Dream That Asked for Space

From the beginning, I knew Marvel 3.0 would not be "another clinic." It had to be an institution — a place where dermatology felt dignified, where learning and healing could coexist.

I was clear about what I wanted:
broad approach roads,
natural light,
visibility,
space for future expansion,
and above all, an institutional presence.

When an estate agent mentioned a plot, I visited it with my father — a ritual shaped by trust and shared judgement. Standing on that land, something felt unmistakably right.

"This is where Marvel will rise," I thought.

At home, Deesha was hesitant. She voiced what any caring partner would:

"Ajay, yeh bahut bada project hai.
Tum stress loge… BP, diabetes ho jayega."

I replied calmly:

"Aakhri step mat socho.
Pehle dekho — kya yeh jagah humare sapne ke laayak hai?"

When Deep and Abhinha ran freely across the open land, laughing, the dream suddenly felt real. Marvel 3.0 had found its place — and its purpose.

The Journal of Possibilities

That night, I opened my journal and wrote down everything honestly:
₹10 lakh in fixed deposits,
₹25 lakh in mutual funds,
the possibility of selling a row house,
a plot in Ambajogai,
my mother offering her gold,
support from Vijay,
and my sister Anjalee ready to help.

Even then, the numbers were short.

And yet, almost miraculously, buyers appeared — for both properties.
Even I, a rationalist, paused.

There was a rhythm to the universe's timing — just as in *The Alchemist.*

Building the Team Behind the Dream

My CA smiled reassuringly:

"Marvel 3.0 will succeed. Loan mil jayega.
Bas paperwork sahi rakho."

Advocate Vaibhav Kulkarni ensured the legal documentation was flawless.

Architect Krishnakumar Bangad of SpaceMagic gave the project its soul.

I have always believed: you grow by the company you keep.
This team strengthened my conviction.

Two Journeys Running Parallel

As Marvel's foundation began to rise, another journey was unfolding — painfully.

Vijay's health declined. I travelled to the USA and stayed with him for two months during surgery. I returned to India heavy-hearted, planning to go back again.

But destiny intervened.

Vijay passed away.

I travelled once more — this time with my father — for the funeral. When I returned to Latur, broken and hollow, Marvel's construction had slowed. Funds were tight. The business loan was delayed. The site stood still.

I had no strength left.

Deesha stepped forward.

She took charge — moving between banks, lawyers, officers, and files. For two relentless months, she held the project together. Finally, the loan was sanctioned.

Marvel 3.0 breathed again.
And slowly, so did I.

Construction, Brick by Brick

Under a detailed turnkey contract with Farhaj Hashmi, construction resumed:
a strong foundation,
wide windows,
spacious OPDs,
soothing interiors,
and a structure that felt calm yet confident.

Every brick reminded me of Vijay. Pride and longing walked together.

The Inauguration — A Day Larger Than Life

After nearly twenty months — delayed by COVID — Marvel 3.0 stood complete.

On the morning of inauguration, the glass façade shimmered softly in sunlight. Nearly five hundred people gathered.

The Chief Guest was **Shri Sanjay Bansode**,
MLA and Minister for Sports & Youth Welfare.

He entered, paused, and absorbed the space. People had expected a clinic. They found an institute — corporate in standards, yet humane in spirit.

Premium architecture.
Glass partitions.
Well-ventilated procedure rooms.
Branding rarely seen in small cities.
In-patient facilities.

Doctors whispered quietly:

"Yeh corporate setup lag raha hai…"

The Minister said:

"Latur ko aise institutions ki zarurat thi.
Ajay, tumne standard hi change kar diya."

When the ribbon was cut, it felt as though a new chapter had opened — not just for me, but for Marathwada.

That evening, I walked alone through the corridors. The air smelled of fresh paint and possibility.

Marvel 3.0 was not magic.
It was discipline taken to its extreme.
Resilience lived daily.
Purpose refused to give up.

A Dream Completed, A Brother Remembered

Standing there quietly, I whispered:

"Vijay should have been here."

Marvel 3.0 carries his influence — in its planning, its systems, its courage.

And in that silence, I felt the familiar voice again:

"Bhau… tu karu shakto."

Marvel 3.0 is more than a clinic.
It is resilience made visible.
A brother's faith carved into architecture.
A family's unity set in stone.

And it marked the beginning
of the next extraordinary chapter of my journey.

CHAPTER 19

Growing With Deesha: Leadership, Empowerment & Identity

Some partnerships are formed by chance.
Some by circumstance.
But the rare ones are forged in fire — tested by uncertainty, shaped by sacrifice, and strengthened by quiet, consistent trust.

Deesha entered my life not as a dramatic turning point, but as a gentle shift — like the first breeze before the monsoon. Soft. Grounding. Full of promise. Her presence never demanded attention; it created stability. And over the years, as life tested us in ways we never anticipated, she transformed from a companion into the steady axis around which my world continued to turn.

The Trials That Tested Her Strength

In the early years of our marriage, Deesha worked as an ad-hoc Assistant Professor in Anatomy. What followed was a phase that would have broken many.

Three times in two years, she received relieving orders when MPSC-selected candidates joined. Three times, she packed her books, her notes, her quiet academic dreams — and walked out with dignity intact.

I remember those evenings clearly. She would return home calm, composed, never bitter. No complaints. No anger.

She would simply say,
"Udya pasun nave sir join hotil."

That calm acceptance, that grace under repeated uncertainty, deepened my respect for her character in a way no words ever could.

A Practical Decision That Changed Everything

After the third termination, we sat together one night — on a simple sofa, children asleep nearby — and spoke honestly about the road ahead.

Our original plan had always been clear:
I would balance private practice with academics.
Deesha would build a long, stable government academic career.

But reality had intervened.

For Deesha to continue in government service, she would need a permanent MPSC post — and that meant leaving Latur, uprooting our young family, and living separately with two small children. That was not a compromise we were willing to make.

So we did something difficult — yet wise.

We reversed our roles.
Not out of defeat.
But out of foresight.

Deesha decided to pursue dermatology through DDV.
I continued my government service.

Our dreams did not change — only the paths did.

That decision quietly altered the trajectory of our lives.

The DDV Journey — Reinvention With Responsibility

The DDV course was demanding. Motherhood was even more so.

At that time, Deep was three years old, and Abhinha just one. Deesha managed the household, cared for the children, and studied late into the night — reading dermatology texts when the house finally fell silent.

Many earn degrees with time and comfort.
She earned hers with responsibility and resilience.

When she completed DDV, it felt less like a qualification and more like a medal — a recognition of perseverance. I carried a pride that words cannot fully capture.

The Partnership That Built Marvel

As Marvel grew — from conversations at the dining table to Marvel 1.0, and later Marvel 3.0 — Deesha was always present.

Not always visible.
But never absent.

She gave clarity when I was overwhelmed.
She questioned me gently when stress clouded judgment.
She celebrated small victories and stood steady during setbacks.

When I doubted whether Marvel 3.0 was too big a dream, she told me quietly:

"Ajay, sapna motha aahe.
Pan tyachya mage tumcha hetu swachha aahe.
He hoil."

Her confidence became my oxygen.

When I Broke — She Carried the Torch

When Vijay fell ill and I travelled to the USA, Marvel 3.0 was still only steel rods and unfinished plans. When Vijay passed away, I returned shattered.

I did not have the strength for files, bank procedures, or documentation. I could not think clearly. I could barely function.

And at that moment, Deesha stepped forward.

She handled bank meetings.
Completed missing documentation.
Followed up relentlessly.
Coordinated with lawyers.
Ensured construction did not stop.

She carried the project not because it was her responsibility — but because it was *ours*.

When the loan was finally sanctioned after two exhausting months, it was her victory. Proof that marriage is not built on romance alone, but on responsibility and trust.

Becoming the Director of Marvel — Identity, Not Title

As a government employee, I could not formally run the clinic. Marvel needed someone who could hold responsibility with legitimacy and competence.

Deesha stepped into that role — not as a technicality, but as a leader.

She mastered accounts, staff management, compliance, scheduling, inventory, patient flow, operations, branding, and long-term planning. Gradually, her thinking began to reflect in every system Marvel built.

Marvel 3.0 — its discipline, precision, and warmth — carries her imprint as much as my vision.

Patients began to recognise her not as "the doctor's wife," but as **Dr. Deesha** — a professional with her own authority and identity. Watching that transformation filled me with quiet pride.

A Marriage of Equality, Not Sacrifice

What defines our journey is not how much we endured, but how much we shared.

We did not compete.
We complemented each other.

We raised children, built careers, faced loss, and created something larger than ourselves — together. Our marriage was never about sacrifice alone.
It was about growth.

The Quiet Strength Behind Marvel

If Marvel 3.0 is my creation, its heartbeat is Deesha.

Behind every system, every decision, every calm resolution, and every structured process stands her quiet strength.

She did not allow grief to paralyse life.
She rebuilt me when I was broken.
She continues to lead with humility and purpose.

A Journey Still Unfolding

Deesha is no longer the young professor facing uncertainty.
She is no longer the student studying at midnight.
She is no longer the partner worried about my stress.

She has grown into:
a leader,
a director,
a dermatologist,
a mother,
a strategist,
and a partner.

Her journey is still unfolding — one decision, one day, one act of strength at a time. And I know this with certainty:

Marvel did not rise because of me alone.
It rose because we rose together.

CHAPTER 20

The Children: Quiet Inspiration Behind Every Decision

There are moments in life when we believe we are shaping our children.
And then there are moments when we realise, with quiet humility, that they are shaping us.

In the long journey of building Marvel, teaching at GMC, rebuilding life after loss, and carrying responsibilities that often felt heavier than words — two small hands, and then four, held my world together.

Their names are **Deep** and **Abhinha**.

They were never just children in my life.
They became sources of energy, direction, clarity — and above all, hope.

Deep — Strength That Speaks Softly

Deep grew up with a rare balance of calmness and ambition. He was never loud, never demanding attention — yet people noticed him naturally.

He is intelligent, social, athletic, disciplined, bold, and fearless. A natural leader who understands situations quickly and stands firmly against injustice. He studies sincerely, learns fast, and carries himself with quiet confidence.

At school, he played football and cricket at competitive levels. He exercised daily, maintained an athletic build, and showed equal interest in music, biology, and mathematics. Wherever he went, friendships followed — effortlessly.

Watching him grow taught me a simple truth:

Strength does not need noise.
It needs purpose.

Abhinha — Curiosity That Lights the Room

If Deep is calm fire, Abhinha is a bright spark.

Joyful, expressive, sharp, and endlessly curious — his teachers affectionately called him *"Google."* Many times, his questions were so perceptive that teachers themselves had to look up answers.

He loved physics and mathematics, created an **Emergency App at the age of seven**, won a **Silver Medal in the Homi Bhabha Junior Scientist Examination**, and earned multiple awards at school, division, and state levels. At eleven, he authored a book titled *"The Mystery of the Golden Stone."* He acted in an advertisement with Hrithik Roshan, learned Spanish through an app, and instinctively understood coding and technology.

Through him, I was reminded of something essential:

Children do not see the world as it is.
They see it as it *can* be.

And that vision reignited my own creativity many times.

The Day They Offered Their Piggy Banks

During the planning of Marvel 3.0, our family sat together — calculating finances, assessing risks, and deciding the future.

In the middle of this serious discussion, Deep and Abhinha quietly walked away. A few minutes later, they returned — each holding a piggy bank.

Deep offered **₹20,000**.
Abhinha offered **₹12,000**.

They looked at us and said simply,
"We want to invest in Marvel."

My throat tightened. Deesha was speechless. Even my parents' eyes filled with emotion.

That day, I realised something profound:

Marvel was no longer just my dream.
It belonged to the entire family.

Witnesses to a Dream Rising from the Ground

Throughout the construction of Marvel 3.0, the entire family visited the site regularly — Deesha, my parents, Deep, Abhinha, my sister Anjalee, and sometimes even my nephew Arohan.

The children watched steel beams rise, walls form, glass panels shine, and rooms emerge from emptiness. They asked thoughtful questions:

"Why is this room so big?"
"Will patients feel comfortable here?"
"How many people will sit in OPD?"
"Where will recovery happen?"

They weren't just observing a building.
They were understanding a vision.

Building Together — One Chair at a Time

When patient chairs arrived from Delhi, they came dismantled — nuts, bolts, rods everywhere.

Instead of calling workers, I smiled and said,
"Let's do it together."

For an entire day, we sat on the floor — my parents, Deesha, Deep, Abhinha, and I — assembling chairs, tightening bolts, sharing tea, laughing.

These moments do something powerful.

They turn buildings into homes.
They turn clinics into institutions.

Children of a Digital Generation

Deep and Abhinha brought modern energy into Marvel.

They helped edit Deesha's YouTube videos, contributed ideas for the website, assisted with digital planning, and understood technology faster than most adults around them.

They grew up watching me plan Marvel in my journal. Today, they help execute those ideas.

This generational continuity is what will one day shape **Marvel 4.0**.

Their Bond with Vijay

Vijay adored the children. Whenever he visited, they clung to him, calling him *"Chachu,"* refusing to leave his side.

He dreamed of taking them to the USA, exposing them to the world, and helping them dream bigger.

When I returned from the USA after being with Vijay, Deep travelled nearly **300 km to Hyderabad airport** just to receive me.

In that moment, I realised how deeply children understand grief — often more profoundly than adults.

Mountains That Strengthened the Family

Every year, our extended family travelled together. But trekking became something special.

Together, we completed:

Beas Kund Trek — 3,700 m (12,139 ft)

Hampta Pass — 4,333 m (14,065 ft)

These were not easy treks. They demanded endurance, courage, and unity.

The children encouraged me to take up trekking, helped plan routes, manage bookings, and stood beside me at every altitude.

Those mountains tested more than our lungs.
They tested our bond — and strengthened it.

The Values I Wanted to Pass On

I always knew what kind of father I wanted to be.

Strict about education.
Strict about healthy habits.
Gentle about everything else.

I wanted them to learn:

Ambedkarite equality,
Buddhist calmness,
self-respect,
compassion,
financial literacy,
entrepreneurship,
leadership,
and humility.

Not through lectures — but through example.

To be **human first**, educated second, successful third.

The Gift They Gave Me

Raising Deep and Abhinha did not just make me a father.
It made me more patient, playful, grounded, disciplined, and fulfilled.

Through them, I lived my childhood again.
Through teaching them values, I reinforced my own.

They were not just children.
They were mirrors — reflecting the best version of myself.

A Family Statement

One evening, we sat together and wrote a family statement — a promise of who we were and who we aspired to be.

It was not a document.
It was a commitment.

A reminder that no matter how large Marvel becomes, no matter how many patients come, no matter how high I rise —

Family will always remain the foundation of every dream.

And Deep and Abhinha are the brightest lights in that foundation.

CHAPTER 21

Becoming Professor: A Journey of Consistency, Character And Quiet Determination

Professorship is not a title.
It is a process of becoming.

It is shaped silently over years — in classrooms, OPDs, ward corridors, late-night rounds, and in the uncelebrated spaces of administration where real leadership is tested. My journey to becoming Professor was not marked by a single signature on a promotion order. It was the cumulative result of consistency, character, and quiet determination.

Shaping Doctors — Long Before the Title

Long before I formally became a Professor, I had already assumed that role in the eyes of my MBBS students.

To me, teaching was never a timetable obligation. It was a responsibility to the profession and to society. I believed that medical education must produce not only competent clinicians, but ethical, rational, and socially sensitive human beings.

In classrooms and OPDs, I focused on more than diagnoses and treatment protocols. I spoke about clinical reasoning, ethical decision-making, scientific temper, compassion, dignity, and self-respect in medical practice.

I encouraged students to question, to debate, to think independently.
I often told them:

"A doctor must be scientifically sharp and socially sensitive."

Many students later told me that what stayed with them was not just dermatology — but perspective.

Building Character, Not Just Careers

Medical knowledge can be acquired from books. Character must be cultivated.

On the birth anniversaries of **Dr. Babasaheb Ambedkar** and **Chhatrapati Shivaji Maharaj**, I initiated programmes for students — not as ceremonial events, but as platforms for reflection and growth.

These included speeches, debates, cultural expressions, and leadership discussions. Through them, I wanted students to understand ideas larger than examinations:

From Ambedkar — rationality, equality, fraternity, constitutional morality, and scientific thinking.
From Shivaji Maharaj — leadership, courage, strategy, accountability, and justice.

I reminded students that a degree gives authority, but character gives legitimacy.

Helping Students Navigate Difficult Systems

Medical education is not confined to textbooks and examinations. It also involves navigating bureaucracy — forms, permissions, stipends, scholarships, documentation, and institutional processes.

Over time, I became someone students approached when they felt stuck — when stipends were delayed, certificates pending, research approvals stalled, or when they simply needed confidence to speak up.

I helped quietly, without expectations. To me, this was not generosity. It was duty.

I believed that if I had reached a position where I could help, then I was obligated to do so.

Developing Leaders, Not Followers

I never wanted my students to be passive recipients of instruction. I wanted them to think, question, analyze, and take responsibility.

I encouraged them to participate in student councils, academic committees, research activities, cultural initiatives, and community health programmes. When they hesitated, I reminded them:

**"Leadership is not about being the loudest.
It is about being the most responsible."**

Over the years, many students went on to excel — in postgraduate entrances, global examinations, dermatology residencies, research, and administrative roles. I celebrated their success quietly, with gratitude rather than pride.

Administrative Responsibility — Without Noise

With time, my approach to work and fairness in decision-making were recognised by the institution. I was entrusted with the role of **Deputy Dean**, and during the Dean's absence, I was given charge of the Dean's office.

This was not ceremonial authority. It meant handling crises, resolving conflicts, maintaining discipline, ensuring academic continuity, and coordinating between departments and government authorities.

I approached administration the same way I approached clinical work — calmly, ethically, and with documentation that spoke clearly.

The Sacrifices Behind the Silence

People see promotions. They rarely see what lies behind them.

They do not see the late nights, the missed family dinners, the emotional burden of dual responsibilities, the pressure of balancing GMC and Marvel, or the discipline required to remain ethical under strain.

I never spoke about these sacrifices. Not because they didn't exist — but because a professor works for impact, not applause.

The Promotion — A Quiet Moment

When the promotion order finally arrived —

Professor, Dermatology
Government Medical College, Latur

I did not celebrate outwardly. I read it once, closed my eyes briefly, and felt a quiet warmth.

I thought of my parents, Deesha, Deep and Abhinha, Vijay, my mentors, my students, the early ST bus days, the long OPDs, the silent persistence.

The promotion did not feel like an achievement.
It felt like a reflection of who I had become.

What Professorship Means to Me

To me, being a Professor means:

shaping future doctors

protecting residents

upholding ethics

preserving constitutional values

mentoring with compassion

maintaining scientific temperament

building institutions

teaching with integrity

leading with humility

I often tell my students:

"Excellence is not an act.
It is a habit."

And quietly, through consistency and commitment, I continue to live by it.

CHAPTER 22

The Marvel Institute: A Vision Beyond a Clinic

Some creations are meant for the present.
Some are meant for the future.
And a rare few are built quietly, with the intention of becoming something much larger than they appear.

Marvel 3.0 was never meant to remain only a clinic.
From the day it took shape, it was designed as a foundation — capable of carrying a dream that would outlive me.

That dream is **The Marvel Institute**.

Not an institute of today,
but an institute of tomorrow —
already alive in purpose,
waiting patiently for the right moment to unfold.

Where the Idea Began — A Thought Waiting for Time

The idea of the Marvel Institute did not arise from ambition, competition, or a desire for prestige.
It grew from a quiet conviction I carried for years:

A clinic should not end with a doctor.
A doctor's work should become a legacy.
And a legacy should inspire others to build.

I had always believed that excellence should not belong only to large cities or privileged institutions. A doctor working honestly in a district town should be able to create systems, standards, and institutions — not just consulting rooms.

I often asked myself:

Why should only metropolitan cities have institutes?
Why not Latur?
Why not us?

The Marvel Institute was conceived as a message — not a declaration — to students, young doctors, and ordinary citizens:

If someone from a small town can build something meaningful with discipline, ethics, and persistence, then greatness is not limited by geography.

No shortcuts.
No inflated claims.
Only consistent effort, ethical work, and belief in oneself.

At its heart, the idea was simple:

To show that ordinary people can create extraordinary outcomes when values guide vision.

Marvel 3.0 — Designed With Tomorrow in Mind

Although the Marvel Institute has not been formally launched, Marvel 3.0 was consciously designed to support education and training in the future.

The layout reflects this intention:

spacious, well-lit procedure rooms

calm, uncluttered interiors

digital-ready infrastructure

architectural flow suitable for demonstrations and discussions

spaces that can easily transform into teaching zones

Visitors often say,
"This feels more like an institute than a clinic."

They are not wrong.

Marvel 3.0 is not the destination.
It is the starting platform.

Public Education — The First Living Wing

While formal training programs have not yet begun, education has already found its way into Marvel.

Through **Deesha's community dermatology sessions**, awareness has reached colleges, women's groups, schools, and youth forums. Topics range from acne science and fungal infection myths to vitiligo awareness, steroid misuse, and adolescent skin health.

Through **Marvel's digital presence**, especially the YouTube channel, dermatology education now travels far beyond Latur — addressing myths, simplifying science, and empowering patients.

Through **newspaper articles and public columns**, we have spoken consistently about skin diseases, leprosy, vitiligo, steroid abuse, and rational skincare.

In this way, the Marvel Institute has already begun — not in classrooms, but in minds.

Training for Doctors — A Vision, Not Yet Activated

I envision a time when dermatologists from across Marathwada will visit Marvel to learn:

laser fundamentals

vitiligo surgery principles

scar and acne management protocols

rational dermatology practice

ethical clinic building

This has not started yet.
And that honesty matters.

But the space is ready.
The intent is clear.
And the vision is steady.

I believe deeply:

First build the foundation.
Then the institute will build itself.

Research and Writing — The Road Ahead

Formal research under the Marvel banner is still part of the future blueprint.

The plan includes:

systematic case documentation

collaborative studies with GMC

digital outcome archives

academic publications

This is not the present reality.
It is a direction — waiting for the right phase.

An institute must grow in stages, not rush its identity.

Why an Institute? Why Here? Why Me?

Because I have seen:

the hunger for knowledge in district students

the lack of advanced exposure outside cities

the burden of myths in dermatology

the need for rational, scientific public education

I believe strongly:

Knowledge should not only flow downward from cities.
It must rise upward from districts as well.

The Marvel Institute is meant to be that upward current.

A Family That Dreams Together

This vision has never been mine alone.

Deesha contributes through education and outreach.
Deep and Abhinha support digital thinking and modern ideas.
My parents and sister have stood beside every decision.

The institute already stands on a foundation of shared values — long before its formal nameplate appears.

Looking Ahead — Without Hurry

The future may hold:

structured workshops

online teaching modules

certificate programs

adolescent skin education initiatives

academic collaborations

small, meaningful conferences in Latur

None of this is happening yet.
And that restraint is deliberate.

Because I know:

A great institute is not inaugurated.
It is prepared, nurtured, and earned.

Marvel 3.0 is that preparation.
The Marvel Institute is the dream.

And someday — when experience meets timing —
it will stand quietly, confidently,
as proof that extraordinary institutions
can rise from ordinary places
when built on discipline, sincerity, and courage.

CHAPTER 23

Building a Department That Will Outlive Me

In government medical colleges, faculty members change, batches pass, and administrative priorities shift.
What remains — and what truly defines a department — is its **culture**.

I have always believed that the role of an academician is not limited to treating patients or completing assigned duties. The real responsibility is to build a department whose strength **deepens with time**, grows with each batch of students, and remains resilient through change.

At forty-seven, with my most productive years ahead, I am not building dermatology at GMC Latur as a closing chapter of my career. I am building it as a **living, evolving system** — one that grows alongside me and continues to rise long after individual milestones fade.

The Early Phase — Seeing Potential Where Others Saw Absence

When I joined GMC Latur, dermatology lacked:

- a structured academic rhythm
- organized documentation
- procedural preparedness
- defined teaching formats
- a shared departmental identity

Many would have accepted these limitations as institutional reality. I saw them as a starting point.

From the beginning, my belief was simple:

Departments grow when people grow.
People grow when systems guide them.

Systems First — The Invisible Strength of a Department

I learned early that institutions do not survive on individual brilliance. They survive on **systems that function independent of personalities**.

Step by step, we built structured frameworks:

- OPD workflows
- standardized documentation registers
- laser and phototherapy protocols
- case presentation formats
- journal club and morbidity review structures
- consent and counselling systems
- procedure room guidelines
- research documentation pathways
- structured teaching schedules for MBBS students and residents

These systems brought stability, predictability, and accountability.

I often tell juniors:

"Individuals change. Systems protect the department."

Creating an Academic Culture — The Soul of the Department

With structure in place, culture followed.

Dermatology at GMC gradually evolved into a vibrant academic unit — not because of size, but because of intent.

We established:

- weekly academic presentations
- structured spotter discussions
- daily clinical reasoning sessions
- interdepartmental case discussions
- active MBBS bedside teaching

Students responded immediately.
Residents engaged deeply.
Learning became participatory, not passive.

Many students later told me:

"Sir didn't just teach dermatology.
He taught us how to think like doctors."

That culture now sustains itself — improving organically with every new batch.

Protecting the Department — Leadership Without Convenience

True leadership appears when personal progress conflicts with institutional interest.

When other departments required additional Associate Professor posts for PG inspections, pressure arose to divert dermatology's sanctioned post. Accepting that would have weakened the department permanently.

I chose otherwise.

I delayed my own promotion by an entire year to protect departmental structure.
I mentored the Assistant Professor closely, ensuring publications were completed ethically so the department could retain its strength.

Only after dermatology's framework was secure did I accept promotion.

My reasoning was clear:

"You do not build a department by surrendering its posts."

That single decision preserved dermatology's academic future for decades.

PG Seats — When a Department Becomes a Legacy

The approval of postgraduate seats marked a defining transformation.

The first inspection was delayed by COVID.
The subsequent inspection succeeded — granting **three MD seats**.
After the first batch passed out, **two additional seats** were sanctioned.

From zero to five seats, dermatology at GMC Latur became a rare example of sustained growth in a district medical college.

I have always believed:

"A department truly becomes an academic institution only when it trains postgraduates."

With PG seats came:

deeper clinical exposure

stronger research potential

improved teaching quality

institutional credibility

The department stepped into a new era.

Laser Advancement — Preparing for Tomorrow's Dermatology

Modern dermatology is incomplete without procedural exposure.

Introducing lasers required patience, documentation, scientific justification, and administrative persistence. But it was essential — not only for PG training requirements, but for patient care and resident skill development.

Today, residents at GMC Latur work with technology once restricted to metropolitan institutions.

That shift redefined the department's future trajectory.

Mentorship — The Most Enduring Contribution

If there is one area I value most, it is mentorship.

Beyond clinical skills, I focus on teaching:

professionalism

ethical documentation

humility

teamwork

communication

scientific temper

Ambedkarite constitutional values

respect for every healthcare worker

I often remind residents:

**"Skill improves outcomes.
Character shapes generations."**

Through mentorship, values outlive individuals.

Administrative Leadership — Seeing Beyond One Department

Over time, my calm approach, fairness, and clarity led to broader administrative roles — including Deputy Dean and Acting Dean responsibilities.

These roles demanded:

crisis management

student advocacy

interdepartmental coordination

institutional discipline

compliance with regulatory bodies

They expanded my perspective from departmental leadership to institutional stewardship.

I learned that:

**"Leadership is not about controlling systems.
It is about refining them."**

A Department Built for the Years Ahead

I am not approaching the end of a career.
I am entering its strongest phase.

The years ahead hold potential for:

research consolidation

procedural expansion

academic collaborations

infrastructure strengthening

increased PG training capacity

deeper community outreach

My focus remains clear:

To build a department where juniors evolve into leaders, systems outlast individuals, and excellence becomes routine.

A Quiet Moment of Realization

One evening, walking toward dermatology OPD, I noticed:

interns discussing cases

residents counselling patients

nurses working confidently

students revising lesions

OPD running smoothly before I entered

And I realized:

**"The department is not growing because of me.
It is growing with me."**

That is the truest measure of academic leadership.

Not a department that survives your absence —
but one that **thrives during your presence** and continues to rise year after year.

I am not building an ending.
I am building momentum.

And the journey ahead is only beginning.

CHAPTER 24

Lessons From 25 Years in Medicine

Twenty-five years in medicine teach you far more about life than about disease.

You begin believing that medicine is about diagnosis, knowledge, and technical skill.
But somewhere along the way, a deeper truth reveals itself:

Medicine is not the study of illness.
It is the study of humanity.

My journey — from a young MBBS student to Professor, department builder, mentor, and founder of Marvel — was shaped not only by clinical experiences, but by people, moments, hardships, and philosophies that slowly sculpted my mind and character.

These are the lessons that stayed.

1. Hardship Is Not Punishment.

It Is Preparation.

The ST bus journeys.
Residency exhaustion.
Limited resources.
Administrative delays.
Emotionally heavy nights.

They were not obstacles.
They were training.

They taught endurance, patience, self-discipline, humility, and clarity of purpose. Those same hardships later became the reason I could carry responsibility calmly and decisively.

When life pushes you,
it is preparing you for higher responsibility.

2. Mentors Can Change Your Destiny

No meaningful journey is solitary.

Undergraduate Mentors

Even before dermatology, two teachers shaped my academic temperament:

Dr. Sahebrao Sadavarte
Dr. Milind Hirwe

They taught discipline, conceptual clarity, scientific reasoning, and the dignity of learning. Their influence became the foundation of my academic life.

Friends Who Shaped My Personality

During MBBS, friendships refined my emotional intelligence and resilience:

Sachin Shinde
Rahul Jawale
Pandurang Raut
Kailas Gaikwad
Anil Palshikar

Through them, I learned teamwork, courage, healthy competition, and loyalty.

We grow through friendships
long before we grow through achievements.

Mentors Beyond Medicine

Two individuals shaped my financial wisdom and stability:

CA Jugal Baheti
CA Shrikant Baheti

They taught me financial discipline, long-term thinking, and ethical decision-making. Marvel 1.0, 2.0, and 3.0 stand firmly on their guidance.

A good CA does not only manage your finances —
he protects your future.

My Mentors

Dr. Hema Jerajani
Dr. Rajeev Joshi
Dr. Shrikant Gore

They shaped my ethics, academic discipline, courage, and professional identity. They did not just teach dermatology — they taught how to stand with integrity.

3. Ethics Is the Only Long-Term Strategy

Medicine offers shortcuts at every turn.

I learned early:
Shortcuts bring quick success,
but destroy quiet sleep.

Long-term respect grows from honesty, transparent communication, avoiding unnecessary procedures, and keeping a clean conscience. Ethics became my compass.

4. Patients Teach More Than Textbooks

Patients taught me empathy, patience, humility, courage, and perspective.

Once a patient said:

*"Doctor, your presence healed me
before your medicine did."*

I never forgot that.

5. Systems Are More Powerful Than Individuals

Individuals may be talented.
Systems create consistency.

**If the system is strong,
the department remains strong —
regardless of who comes or goes.**

This lesson shaped every administrative decision I made.

6. Leadership Requires Sacrifice

I delayed my own promotion to protect departmental posts.
I fought for PG seats, laser procurement, and academic fairness.

Leadership is not convenience.

Leadership is courage.

7. No One Succeeds Alone

— Family Is the Greatest Strength**

Every milestone was touched by:

Deesha
My children
My parents
My brother Vijay
Mentors

Well-wishers
Extended family

The world sees achievements.
Family sees the journey.

8. Loss Is a Teacher More Powerful Than Success

Losing Vijay reshaped my worldview — deepening gratitude, compassion, and acceptance.

**Loss breaks you,
then rebuilds you wiser.**

9. Teaching Is the Purest Form of Service

When a student says,

"Sir, you changed how I think,"

that becomes the highest reward.

**A teacher lives through those
he has taught.**

10. Leadership Is Behaviour,

Not Designation

Through roles as Deputy Dean and Acting Dean, I learned:

Leadership is fairness, calmness, clarity, accountability, and empathy.

**A leader improves systems
without seeking applause.**

11. Medicine May Not Be Perfect,

But Your Conduct Can Be

Even when systems fail,
Work with integrity —
especially when no one is watching.

12. Success Grows Silently

Marvel 3.0 did not rise through noise.
It rose through discipline, values, patience, planning, courage, and family.

Quiet success lasts longest.

13. Gratitude Is the Highest Intelligence

Gratitude keeps achievement grounded and struggle meaningful.

14. Dreams Are Built

Slowly, Consistently, Truthfully

Marvel grew through years of planning, saving, discussion, journaling, execution, and belief.

Dreams unfold only when dedication becomes habit.

15. The Journey Is the Real Reward

Looking back, the most meaningful moments were not outcomes, but effort, growth, struggle, and relationships.

Medicine gave me not just a career,
but a life of purpose.

And the journey continues.

CHAPTER 25

Love, Loss & What Life Ultimately Teaches Us

There comes a time in every life
when achievements fade into the background,
when titles stop mattering,
and what remains is simply
who stood with you
and who you became through it all.

Love, loss, and time have a way of revealing
the deepest truths of our journey.

My life—with all its layers of medicine, Marvel, GMC, and leadership—
ultimately returns to one centre:

family, values, resilience, impermanence, and gratitude.

The most profound lessons I have learned
did not come from textbooks, conferences, or institutions.
They came from people who were shaping me quietly,
long before I understood what strength truly meant.

This chapter belongs to them.

The Love That Raised Me — My Parents and My Sister

Before the world shaped me,
I was shaped at home
by three people who built me
with softness, discipline, and unwavering belief:
my mother, my father, and my sister, Anjalee.

If everything I have built today stands upright,
it is because they held me upright
long before society noticed my existence.

My Mother — The Quiet Strength Behind Every Step

My mother lived her life
like a silent prayer in motion.

Married early into a large joint family,
with responsibilities far beyond her age,
she carried the burdens of a home
with the gentleness of someone
who accepts duty as devotion.

Beneath that gentleness lived quiet fire.

After marriage and motherhood,
she pursued her education—
D.Ed., B.A., M.A.,M.Ed—
and became a primary school teacher
travelling daily to a Zilla Parishad village school.
She retired as Headmistress,
her journey carved through sacrifice, discipline, and belief.

My love for books—
the habit of reading, thinking, questioning—
came from her hands.
Our home was filled with charts, storybooks, workbooks,
and more importantly, with the conviction
that education could rewrite destiny.

During all those years,
she prepared my meals,
packed my tiffin for long ST bus journeys,
and listened patiently to every struggle.
She celebrated my smallest victories
and reassured me during my deepest doubts.

When Marvel 1.0 was only an idea,
she supported it instinctively.
While my father weighed practical concerns,
she said simply:
"You do it. You will do it well."

She handled early Marvel collections,
managed marriage preparations when I was overwhelmed,
and became the one voice
whose appreciation felt like oxygen.

At the inauguration of Marvel 1.0,
when emotion overtook me and tears filled my eyes,
hers mirrored mine—
a silent exchange between a mother and son
who had walked the same road of struggle.

Her tenderness extended naturally to Deesha,
whom she welcomed as a daughter,
supported fully,
and partnered in parenting after retirement.
Deep, Abhinha, and even Arohan
call her *Aai*—
and that says everything.

During Vijay's illness,
she displayed courage beyond language.
When only I could travel to the USA under NIE permission,
she waited anxiously.
Later, when routes opened,
she travelled alone—with Anjalee and Arohan—
navigating international travel for the first time,
staying six months by Vijay's side
with strength that felt almost superhuman.

During Marvel 3.0,
she sold her gold
and contributed from her retirement savings.
Quietly, without telling me,

she contacted Vijay and Anjalee
to support the project.

Her belief in me was never loud.
It was foundational.

My Father — Discipline, Principles, and the Backbone of My Journey

My father was born into poverty—
six siblings, illiterate parents, almost no opportunities.

Yet he carved his life with precision.

He completed his B.Sc. and B.Ed.,
joined Government Medical College, Ambajogai,
as a Laboratory Technician,
and became everything I admired:

disciplined
rational
principled
honest
fearless
financially wise
deeply Ambedkarite

Our home was filled with Babasaheb Ambedkar's writings.
From him, I learned constitutional morality,
equality, dignity, and rational thought.

He ensured I never lacked during MBBS—
supported me financially,
gifted me a bike on graduation,
and later, seeing my exhausting ST bus routine,
gifted me my first car
because he could no longer watch my hardship.

When Marvel 1.0 was conceived,
he worried—not from doubt,
but from a lifetime lived close to poverty.
Yet once I decided,
he stood beside me firmly.

He accompanied me to Latur,
helped select the space,
and mortgaged our Ambajogai home
to finance the dream.

For Marvel 3.0,
he contributed from his retirement funds,
sold his long-held plot,
guided legal processes, documentation, contracts, and construction.
He supervised Marvel
as if it were his own creation—
because it was.

At Marvel 3.0's inauguration,
his pride was unmistakable.

Today, at 73—healthy, addiction-free—
he lives with us,
managing staff, supervising pharmacy operations,
guiding finances, bonding with the children,
joining family trips,
living with dignity and routine.

When Vijay was diagnosed,
he carried his grief silently
to support all of us.
He travelled with me to the USA for the funeral—
his first international journey—
a father's strength walking beside his son.

If my mother is my emotional foundation,
my father is the structure, discipline, and clarity
on which my life stands.

My Sister — Anjalee: Gentle Heart, Unbreakable Spirit

My sister, Dr. Anjalee,
is the tenderest part of our family—
and one of its strongest.

Calm, sensitive, introverted, deeply compassionate,
she lives by Buddha's values:
pradnya (wisdom), *sheel* (character), *karuna* (compassion).

She completed MBBS in the same college as I did;
those two shared years forged an unbreakable bond.
During her PG-CET preparation,
I gave her my debit card—
she used it with integrity and restraint
that reflected her character.

She completed MD Anatomy from KEM, Mumbai,
and today is a Professor—
a beloved teacher
and contributor to CBME and modern pedagogy.

She shares deep affection with Deesha,
a special bond with Deep and Abhinha,
and unwavering love for Arohan.

During Vijay's illness,
she called daily, guided diet, searched treatment options,
and kept me informed continuously.
She travelled to the USA with our mother
through quarantine and uncertainty,
and after Vijay's passing,
stood with me through unbearable silence.

At the same time,
she faced personal storms of her own—
rebuilding life alone,
protecting her son,
standing with dignity.

During Marvel 3.0,
when she sensed financial strain,
she transferred support immediately—
without being asked,
without ever mentioning it again.

She is not just my sister.
She is the emotional extension of my strength—
the one who understands silence.

What Life Ultimately Teaches Us

Life teaches you that
love does not need loud declarations—
it needs presence.

It teaches you that
loss is not an end—
it is the beginning of deeper understanding.

It teaches you that
resilience is carried quietly
by those who stand behind you,
not beside your achievements.

It teaches you that
family is not defined only by blood,
but by those who walk with you
from ST bus struggles
to international hospitals,
from dreams

to grief
to grace.

And it teaches you this final truth:

Without them—
Marvel, GMC, and this book
would not exist.

CHAPTER 26

Epilogue: My Marvellous Journey Continues

A book ends.
But a life—especially a life built on purpose—never truly does.

As I stand today, looking at everything life has given me,
everything it has taken,
everything it has shaped,
and everything it continues to promise,
one truth becomes clear:

My journey has never been about achievements.
It has always been about becoming.

Becoming stronger.
Becoming wiser.
Becoming kinder.
Becoming more aware.
Becoming more human.

These pages capture the years behind me.
But the most meaningful chapters
are still waiting to be written.

The Road Ahead — Growth, Responsibility, Purpose

I am not at the end of my career.
I am in its strongest, most responsible phase.

Ahead of me lie years of meaningful work:

strengthening my department

shaping generations of students

mentoring young dermatologists

expanding Marvel

nurturing the vision of the Marvel Institute

deepening community education

contributing to research and digital learning

raising my children into thoughtful global citizens

building a legacy grounded in values, not vanity

I am not slowing down.
I am stepping more consciously into my purpose.

A Message to My Children — Deep & Abhinha

To Deep and Abhinha—
who gave meaning to every sacrifice
and unknowingly taught me how to live with joy—

You have been my greatest teachers.
You helped me grow more than any degree ever could.

If there is one inheritance I wish to leave you,
it is this:

self-respect

compassion

discipline

curiosity

courage to walk your own path

scientific temper

constitutional values

Dream big.
Work honestly.
Do not fear difficulty.
Do not compromise your truth.

Be good human beings first.
Everything else will follow.

A Message to My Students

Students have always been the quiet heartbeat of my journey.

To each of you, I say this:
Knowledge is important.
But character is everything.

Learn to:

think rationally

practise ethically

treat patients with dignity

question unscientific beliefs

lead with humility

protect those junior to you

respect every member of the healthcare system

Remember:
A good doctor treats disease.
A great doctor serves society.

A Message to Young Doctors and Readers

To those standing at the beginning of their journey—
unsure, anxious, hopeful—

Do not fear starting small.
Do not fear hard work.
Do not fear standing alone for what is right.
Do not fear dreaming big from a small place.

I built Marvel brick by brick,
day by day,
without shortcuts,
guided by sincerity.

If my life carries one message, it is this:

Ordinary people can create extraordinary things
when they work with ethics, courage, and purpose.

A Message to Society

Medicine is not confined to hospitals.
It belongs to society.

It stands for:

awareness

rationality

equality

compassion

responsibility

The values of Babasaheb Ambedkar
and the calm wisdom of Buddha
remind me daily that:

dignity is non-negotiable

science is essential

humility is strength

Society progresses
when individuals act with clarity and kindness.

A Message to Myself

If I could speak to my younger self—
the boy from Latur,
the exhausted MBBS student,
the resident on monsoon nights,
the young doctor dreaming of Marvel,
the grieving brother learning to stand again—

I would say only this:

You stayed honest.
You stayed human.
You did well.
Keep going.

And if I speak to my future self—
years from now—
I hope to say:

I remained grounded.
I served sincerely.
I built something meaningful.

The Final Thought

This book is not the conclusion of my story.
It is only a pause—
a reflection.

Ahead lie:
new students
new responsibilities
new innovations
new challenges
new dreams
new lessons
new chapters for Marvel
new phases of family life

I walk forward with:
gratitude in my heart,
clarity in my mind,
and purpose in my work.

My marvellous journey continues.

Acknowledgments

No meaningful journey is ever walked alone.
This book may carry my name, but it is shaped by the presence, guidance, and quiet support of many.

I express my deepest gratitude to my **mentors and teachers—Dr. Hema Jerajani, Dr. Rajeev Joshi, and Dr. Shrikant Gore**—whose influence shaped my clinical thinking, ethics, and leadership. I am equally thankful to my undergraduate mentors **Dr. Sahebrao Sadavarte** and **Dr. Milind Hirwe**, who laid the foundation of my academic discipline.

I acknowledge **Government Medical College, Latur**, and my colleagues, residents, nurses, Class IV staff, and administrative teams, whose collective effort made departmental growth and academic culture possible.

My sincere thanks to **CA Jugal Baheti** and **CA Shrikant Baheti** for their financial wisdom, ethical guidance, and unwavering support through every phase of Marvel Clinic.

I am grateful to **Mr. Krishnakumar Bangad (Architect, SpaceMagic)** for giving Marvel 3.0 its institutional soul through thoughtful design, and to **Mr. Farhaj Hashmi (Contractor)** for executing the vision with integrity, discipline, and professionalism.

I thank **Sumit Sonkusare**, my brother-in-law, for designing the logo and visual identity of Marvel Clinic.

I thank friends and well-wishers—especially **Dr. Bharat Sonawane** and **Dr. Umesh Kanade**—whose help came not as obligation, but as genuine goodwill.

I offer heartfelt gratitude to my **parents**, **Govind Ovhal** and **Suvarnalata Ovhal** whose sacrifices built the foundation of my life, and to my **father-in-law and mother-in-law**, for their warmth, understanding, and quiet support that strengthened our family through demanding years.

To my **students**, I owe a special debt. Teaching you refined my own thinking and reaffirmed my belief that education is a responsibility, not a privilege. To my **patients**, thank you for your trust—your lives taught me lessons no textbook could.

Above all, I acknowledge my **family**—my sister Anjalee, my wife Deesha, and my children Deep and Abhinha—who transformed ambition into purpose. And to my brother **Vijay**, whose belief in me continues to guide my steps.

If this book carries any truth, it is because many walked beside me when the path was uncertain.

About the Author

Dr. Ajay Ovhal is a dermatologist, academician, institution builder, and lifelong learner, whose journey has been shaped as much by discipline and service as by reflection and resilience.

Born and raised in rural Maharashtra, his life did not begin with privilege, but with values—education earned through effort, stability built through patience, and dreams protected through quiet determination. From navigating long ST bus journeys during his early career to building Marvel Clinic brick by brick, his path has been one of steady progress rather than sudden success.

Dr. Ovhal is currently a Professor of Dermatology at Government Medical College, Latur, where he has played a pivotal role in transforming a once-neglected department into a structured, academically active, postgraduate centre. His work spans clinical dermatology, teaching, administration, and mentorship, with a strong emphasis on ethics, systems, and long-term institutional growth.

Alongside government service, he founded Marvel Clinic, which evolved from a modest 360 sq ft setup into Marvel 3.0—an institute-level practice that reflects his belief that excellence should not be limited to metropolitan cities. His vision extends beyond practice into education, community awareness, and the gradual development of the Marvel Institute.

Deeply influenced by Ambedkarite values and Buddhist philosophy, Dr. Ovhal believes that medicine is ultimately a moral profession—one that demands rational thinking, compassion, dignity, and responsibility toward society. He is known among students and colleagues for his calm leadership, clarity of thought, and commitment to building systems that outlive individuals.

Rising Before the Start Line is his first book

www.ingramcontent.com/pod-product-compliance
Lightning Source LLC
Chambersburg PA
CBHW050016170726
48282CB00025B/426
* 9 7 8 9 3 5 6 2 6 0 1 2 2 *